THE FINAL WITNESS

THE FINAL WITNESS

A KENNEDY
SECRET SERVICE
AGENT BREAKS
HIS SILENCE
AFTER 60 YEARS

PAUL LANDIS

CHICAGO
REVIEW
PRESS

First hardcover edition published in 2023
First paperback edition published in 2024
Published by Chicago Review Press Incorporated
814 North Franklin Street
Chicago, Illinois 60610
ISBN 978-0-89733-106-7

The Library of Congress has cataloged the
hardcover edition under the following Control
Number: 2023938856

Cover design: Preston Pisellini
Cover photo: Bettman/Getty Images
Typesetting: Nord Compo

Printed in the United States of America

To Freedom
and the continuous search
for Truth and Peace

CONTENTS

ACKNOWLEDGMENTS

WHERE TO BEGIN saying *thank you* is easy, but where to stop is not. So many people have helped me write this book, some providing one-word answers to specific questions, others offering lengthy how-to lessons, and many encouraging me to tell my story. There is a special place in my heart for all of you, and I can't thank you enough. If I've omitted your name in these acknowledgments, it's only because there isn't enough room to call out the names of everyone who has been there for me.

Before the first words of this book were ever written, I looked for assurance that I had a story to tell. Lew Merletti, who was director of the Secret Service during the Clinton administration, met me for lunch one day, and I trusted him with my story. He emphasized to me that my story should have been told "like yesterday." He arranged for me to meet with Ken Gormley, who at the time was dean of the School of Law at Duquesne University. (He is now the university's president.) Ken has written several books and had interviewed Lew for *Death of American Virtue: Clinton vs. Starr*. Lew trusted him. Ken agreed with Lew that my story needed to be told, and told "like yesterday." Special thanks go to Ed Cochran, my attorney and friend, who drove me to Pittsburgh, where we met with Ken Gormley at Duquesne. Ed was there at the beginning of this project with encouragement and guidance.

Thank you, Clint Hill. You had confidence in me when you brought me onto the First Lady Detail in October 1962, and we've been friends ever since. I appreciate your support for my book.

This book could never have been realized without the help of my friend Holly Witchey. Holly wears a lot of hats. She is currently the executive director of ICA-Art Conservation, but primarily she is a friend. When we met, we were colleagues at the Western Reserve Historical Society (WRHS) in Cleveland. Holly was a researcher embedded in the Wade family papers in the research library, and I was a security officer. WRHS was undergoing a renovation, and I happened to be seated by a temporary entrance—keeping a sharp eye out for intruders, of course—when Holly walked in. I was jotting down some notes for this book on a pad, and Holly asked me what I was up to. I told her I was having a problem getting started, and she suggested we talk about it over a lunch across the street at the Cleveland Botanical Garden. On Friday, October 27, 2017, we met and the seeds for this book were planted.

Holly volunteered to help me with the project however she could. She told me she would not do any writing—that was my job. She would only guide me through the process. This was a real blessing, because I was a lame duck when it came to using a computer. Holly assured me that my book would be written in my voice and my voice only. No one else could tell my story like I could. *Perfect*, I thought. On November 20, 2017, we had our first meeting.

Over the next three years, Holly and I met nearly every Saturday morning. During the week, I got up at 5:00 AM eastern standard time and wrote before I had to leave for work. On Saturday mornings, Holly would arrive and review what I had written. She then took a printout home for her husband, Curt, to review and edit. On the following Saturday, Holly returned and we repeated the process. I lost track of how many hours we spent together, but it reached the point that one of my neighbors asked her one Saturday if she had moved into the neighborhood. Holly, this book would never have reached completion without you. I am forever indebted and grateful.

In addition to Holly, I had Katryn Duly, my high-octane friend, by my side. Katryn is undoubtedly one of the most intelligent, creative, and energetic persons I have ever known. Her enthusiasm over my book and willingness to help was unmatched. She rescued me countless times on my computer. Katryn, you are a blessing and a true friend.

Phi Alpha to Evan Corns. Evan is a Sigma Alpha Epsilon fraternity brother from Ohio Wesleyan University. Evan appeared when I thought I was at a dead end with my book. The two of us were having lunch at Yours Truly Restaurant in Chagrin Falls, Ohio. Our conversation led to Jeff Shaara, author of several historical novels. Evan told me that Jeff was a casual acquaintance, and he wondered whether I would be OK if he reached out to Jeff to see if he could help. Jeff directed me to the man who became my literary agent, Doug Grad. Doug is an extraordinary individual. He took me under his wing after an internet handshake. Doug, you helped me fine-tune my book proposal and you found a publisher willing to take a chance. I can't thank you enough. Thank you, thank you, thank you!

Jerome "Jerry" Pohlen, Senior Editor at Chicago Review Press, was willing to roll the dice and take a chance on me after reading my book proposal, and here we are today.

Devon Freeny, my editor, was absolutely superb to work with. Devon, you were so meticulous about the details in my book that you immediately earned my confidence. Thank you for helping me put the finishing touches on my manuscript and guiding me through the process. You are definitely a winner and a dream come true for any writer.

As I mentioned above, many people responded to my story and my requests for information. Author and film producer Glenn Palmedo-Smith had an idea for a book and film years ago. He was persistent, but I just wasn't ready to write. The other individuals who provided help and information include: Norb Cygan, Art Greenberg, David Eisenhower, the archivists and staff at the Kennedy Library in Boston (Stacey Chandler, Maryrose Grossman, Laurie Austin, and Abigail Malangone), Nicola Longford and Stephen Fagin at the Sixth Floor Museum in Dallas, and Grayce Rogers at the JFK Hyannis Museum in Hyannis, Massachusetts.

Sadly, there are two special people who are no longer here to thank: Bob Foster, who started me on the road to becoming a Secret Service agent, and Shaker Heights police chief D. Scott Lee, who fifty-six years later started me on the path to this book.

I want to thank my two children, Jenni Robinson and Tom Landis, for their patience over the years. I never took the opportunity to share all my stories or why I left the Secret Service. Now they know.

And last but definitely not least, I have to honor and thank Mary Jo Nigro, my companion and significant other for the past thirty years. She has been with me every step of the way and has had infinite patience as I disappeared downstairs to write, and write, and write. MJ, I am especially grateful for your love and support.

INTRODUCTION

DECEMBER 14, 2013, was the kind of day most Northeast Ohioans expect at that time of year. Crisp and cool outside with the temperatures in the lower thirties and a gray canopy of winter clouds overhead. *Well,* I thought to myself as I left the house, *at least it isn't snowing.* I was heading to the police station to help with the annual bicycle/property auction.

Ten years earlier I had attended the Shaker Heights Citizens Police Academy, a course offered by the police department to help community members learn how their local police force operates. Police officers introduce attendees to all aspects of the department's operations, and by the end of the course attendees have a fairly full picture of what is involved in keeping their community safe. After completing the course, graduates are invited to join Shaker Heights' Citizens Police Association (CPA). If they are interested enough, after a background check, CPA members can volunteer to help with various police activities. I helped with weapons cleaning and with the annual bicycle/property auction.

The auction was being held in the drive-through garage attached to the back of the police station. On that day, it was about two-thirds full of abandoned bicycles, and the garage doors were open at both ends. A cold breeze blew through, but we were sheltered in case of snow.

In spite of the temperature, more than two dozen people showed up that day. It was known to be a great place to pick up a used bicycle at a bargain price. We'd set up a table and an auctioneer stand. My job, once we got underway, was to lift a bicycle up onto the table beside the auctioneer so that everyone could get a good look and start bidding.

We were about an hour into the auction when someone called, "Hey Paul, the chief wants to see you." I turned around and saw Chief D. Scott Lee (1959–2016) standing by the rear entrance. He motioned for me to come over, so I stopped what I was doing and asked another volunteer to take my place.

Chief Lee was wearing casual clothes: sneakers, well-worn blue jeans, a gray sweatshirt, and a tan fleece-lined windbreaker with the Shaker Heights Police Department logo. It was Saturday, his day off, but he had stopped by the station just to see how the auction was going. I liked Chief Lee and was pleased to see him there. It showed his commitment to the job and proved his interest in and support for our organization. But as I walked over to the chief, making my way through the rows of unsold bicycles, I wondered what was up, and why on earth he wanted to see me.

Little did I know that those few short steps would set me on the journey to this book. We greeted each other with a warm handshake, and Chief Lee said, "Follow me."

We entered the station and walked past a classroom on the right where everyone had previously assembled for coffee and donuts. (It's a police station, after all!) We got to his office and Chief Lee went directly to a bookshelf, pulled out a book, and handed it to me. "Here," he said. "I want you to have this. It was sent to me by a good friend. When I received it, I immediately thought of you."

The colors on the book's cover were a faded red and blue. The binding was brittle and coming apart, and the pages were dried and stiff. The book had a strong musty odor, and I sensed that it had been long forgotten in a damp basement somewhere for quite some time. No title was visible on the front cover, only four embossed images that reminded me of the crosshairs you see when you look through a telescopic rifle scope. I turned the book sideways so I could read the words printed on the spine: *Six Seconds in Dallas.* I felt a rush of adrenaline, and my heart began to race as I opened the book's cover and read the subtitle: "A Micro-Study of the Kennedy Assassination," by Josiah Thompson.

Almost everyone in the police department knew that I had been in the Secret Service, but only a few, including Chief Lee, knew that I had actually witnessed the assassination of President John F. Kennedy. And none of them knew how witnessing that event had impacted my life. The fact that I had never seen or even heard of this book came as no surprise to me. In the fifty years since President Kennedy's assassination, I had actively avoided reading any books about the events of November 22, 1963.

I thanked Chief Lee, accepted the book, and left the office to return to the bicycle auction. As I passed the classroom, I ducked inside and placed the book on a corner table, thinking it would be safe there until after the auction. It wasn't until I was pulling into my driveway later that afternoon that I realized I'd forgotten Chief Lee's gift. I immediately turned around and headed back to the police station.

The station was only about five minutes from my house, but in the brief amount of time that I was away, someone had already cleaned the classroom, *and my book was gone!* All of the volunteers had left the station, and there were only a couple of officers remaining. Maybe the chief had noticed it, picked it up, and returned it to his office for safekeeping, I hoped.

I cannot begin to explain the anxiety I felt that weekend. I tried to keep positive, thinking that the book would have to turn up. The irony of the entire situation was that in all the years since President Kennedy's assassination I had only read one book about it, *The Kennedy Detail,* by Jerry Blaine and Lisa McCubbin (2010). Now I was obsessed with this old, musty book that had come into my hands and that I had almost immediately misplaced.

On Monday morning I returned to the police station. The officer on duty let me in, and I again headed down the hallway toward the chief's office. I did not have an appointment, and when I reached his office, his secretary advised me that the chief was in a meeting. I told her that I only needed a few seconds with him and said that if it was OK, I would wait outside the office in the hallway, just in case.

While waiting in the hallway I noticed that Debbie Messing, the recreation specialist for the City of Shaker Heights, was in her office. I wandered over to chat. When she asked me why I was there, I started into my tale of woe. She reached over and picked up a book from her desk and asked, "Is this what you are looking for? I found it in the classroom when I was cleaning up after Saturday's auction. I had no idea where it came from, so I just picked it up and put it on my desk."

I could have hugged and kissed Debbie right on the spot. Instead, I thanked her profusely and left the station. Driving home, I was elated. The book was sitting on the passenger seat right there beside me. This was my lucky day. Everything had fallen into place. I had been at the right place at the right time. Somehow, I knew I was meant to have this book. I just felt that somehow it was destined to be in my possession. But why?

When I reached home, I immediately went to the bedroom before removing my coat. I cleared some space on the walnut nightstand next to my bed and placed the book on top of the table. I intended to start reading it that very evening before going to bed.

The evening came and went, then another and another. In fact, about *ninety* evenings came and went, and the book slowly disappeared under copies of *Consumer Reports* and *American Rifleman*. I wanted to read the book, and yet I didn't want to read it. On and on I procrastinated. It had now been over fifty years since President Kennedy's assassination. *Come on, Paul,* I kept telling myself. *The past is history. This is now.* But still I didn't want to read about it.

Finally, one night I crawled into bed, settled in, reached over, and picked up *Six Seconds in Dallas*. It was March 14, 2014, three months to the day since I received the book from Chief Lee. It wasn't long before I became engaged in the book and found myself thinking that this was a fairly accurate description of the events of November 22, 1963. At least it was pretty much how I remembered them. I then came to a point in the book and read something that startled me.

Wait a minute, I thought. I stopped and read it again. *This is wrong. This is not right. This is not the way it was.* I tried reading more, but I was too anxious. My heart was palpitating so fast I couldn't concentrate. I had to stop reading and put the book down. All sorts of thoughts began whirling through my mind. *What to do? Who can I call? What do I say? Who will believe me?* I couldn't sleep.

After a restless night, I got up the next morning and started making notes for this book.

RESIGNATION
AND REFLECTION

United States Secret Service
May 6, 1964

Chief
SA Landis—White House Detail
Resignation

It is respectfully requested that I be granted permission to terminate my employment with the United States Secret Service at the end of the pay period ending August 15, 1964.

It is further requested that I be placed on annual leave commencing June 22, 1964 (OM dated 5-6-64, to SAIC Behn) and that said leave continue until my resignation date.

I no longer have any interest or enthusiasm with regards to my employment, and I feel that by continuing I will only become a liability to the good name which the Secret Service has spent so many years in acquiring.

Paul E. Landis, Jr.
Special Agent

COASTED TO A STOP in front of the heavy, black wrought-iron
gate at the south end of West Executive Avenue, the drive that
separates the White House from the Executive Office Building.
I recognized the guard on duty by his face, but for the life of
me I could not think of his name. I waved and waited for the
gate to open to exit the White House grounds. He returned the
wave and stepped out of the white security booth where he had
been standing. I could not help but notice how sharp he looked
today. He was wearing the standard White House Police uniform, but today his white shirt appeared crisper, the black slacks
seemed to have a sharper crease, and his black shoes looked
shinier than usual. His brass White House Police badge even
seemed to sparkle more.

It's got to be my mood, I thought. I was looking at things
differently, seeing things differently, thinking things differently,
things that until now I hadn't taken much time to think about.
How sad. I had been through this gate many times before when
this same guard was on duty, and now I couldn't even remember
his name. It wasn't like me. What was going on?

The gate was now open, and I was ready to exit. I waved again,
dropped into first gear, and eased my 1962 maroon Corvette convertible onto E Street heading west.

At Twenty-First Street I drove the four blocks south to Constitution Avenue, passing the State Department building along
the way. After reaching Constitution Avenue I turned right, and
then two blocks later at Twenty-Third Street, I made another
left turn. The Lincoln Memorial was straight ahead. I had zig-
zagged my way this far, and my next objective was to cross over
the Potomac River via the Arlington Memorial Bridge. I drove
around Mr. Lincoln and onto the bridge, heading for my apartment in Arlington, Virginia. Ahead of me, at the other end of

the bridge, was Arlington National Cemetery, and I could see Arlington House majestically overlooking the cemetery.

Wow, I thought, *So much history, so much tradition.* My daily drive to and from work took me this way, but it, too, had become a habit, a routine that I had come to take for granted, paying closer attention to traffic than the surrounding landscape and buildings. Now it was midafternoon, traffic was light, and my mind started to wander.

"Mommy, who lives in that big white house up on the hill?" Caroline asked.

A memory from an earlier time had popped into my head. We were heading north on the George Washington Memorial Parkway, returning to the White House after a day trip to some-place—I can't remember where. I was driving one of the black Ford sedans from the White House motor pool. First Lady Jacque-line Kennedy and her daughter Caroline were riding in the back-seat. We had just passed the Pentagon when Arlington National Cemetery came into view, and that's when Caroline spoke up and asked her mother the question.

"Oh, Caroline," Mrs. Kennedy replied. "That is a very famous house. No one lives there now, but it once belonged to a nice man who was a great army general." Mrs. Kennedy then proceeded to explain the history of Arlington House, the mansion that once belonged to General Robert E. Lee, and how the property was now used as a cemetery for select military service members. She did this in such a way that a five-year-old preschooler could under-stand. I was impressed.

BEEP! BEEP!

A car horn honked. I returned to the present. My mind had drifted, and so had my car. *Pay attention Paul*, I thought. *Pay attention.*

I was only about halfway across the bridge when my mind began to wander again. I started thinking about the Tomb of the Unknown Soldier, which was also visible in the distance.

Click, click, click, twenty-one times, stop;
turn around; pause twenty-one seconds; repeat.
Click, click, click, twenty-one times, stop;
turn around; pause twenty-one seconds; repeat.

The heels of the guard on duty at the Tomb of the Unknown Soldier click on the pavement twenty-four hours straight, seven days a week, 365 days a year, year in and year out. Rain, sleet, or snow never interrupts this routine. The only time it is interrupted is during the changing of the guard, which happens every thirty minutes. The whole routine then resumes until the next relief. There is much more behind the symbolism, sacrifices, and commitments of these dedicated warriors, but that's a whole other story in itself.

Then of course there's the Eternal Flame. The flame that also burns 24-7. That flame up on the hill, below and in front of Arlington House, overlooking Arlington Cemetery and Washington, DC. The flame that marks the grave site of former president John F. Kennedy. That flame had haunted me for the past six months. I had been to the Eternal Flame before—I was there when the flame was first lit. I stood by as President Kennedy was laid to rest. I stood by when AF 26000, piloted by Colonel James Swindal, flew overhead, dipping its wings in a final salute to our thirty-fifth President. *Wow!* What an emotional day that had been.

By now I had reached the end of the bridge and was starting to loop around the exit leading onto the Jefferson Davis Highway. My eyes were getting watery and blurry. The top was down on my Corvette, but it wasn't helping to keep my head clear. The tears weren't from the wind. I wiped them away with the back of my hand. I was on the final leg to my apartment located in the Crystal House, the first of two apartment buildings that were the beginning of the Crystal City neighborhood of Arlington. Only five minutes to go and I would stop thinking about the flame. Yeah, right! I couldn't stop thinking about that damn flame and what I had just done. Had I just blown not only my career but also my future—my life?

I was only twenty-eight years old at the time. I was single and had a dream job that I absolutely loved. My job involved travel, excitement, and responsibility, exactly the things I thrived on. I was a special agent (SA) in the United States Secret Service. At the time, I was also serving on a protection detail, which is exactly where I wanted to be. I was proud of my job and especially proud of my current assignment, protecting Mrs. Jacqueline Kennedy, one of the most elegant women in the world. I had been a part of this same detail when Mrs. Kennedy was still the First Lady of the United States. It was definitely a glamorous assignment.

I worked with Special Agent Clinton J. Hill. Clint had been assigned to Mrs. Kennedy since day one, when John F. Kennedy was elected president in November 1960. Along the way, changes were made to her detail, and on March 21, 1962, Clint assumed full command. Clint was the lone agent assigned to Mrs. Kennedy for the next six and a half months, until October 1962, when he asked that I be transferred to join him. The two of us had been working together since then, and we had been through a lot together, both good times and bad. He had become my best friend, and together we were "the First Lady Detail."

Mrs. Kennedy was an absolute pleasure to be around. She was young and vivacious and had a vibrant personality. This made our job more interesting and kept us on our toes. Everyone knew of her beauty, charm, and grace, but she was a real person, with an impish sense of humor. As the wife of the president of the United States, she never smoked in public, but she enjoyed an occasional secret smoke. Clint described one such instance in his book *Mrs. Kennedy and Me*, when Mrs. Kennedy bummed a cigarette from him and they shared a smoke in her limo.

I remember one particular example of her mischievousness and sense of fun. Clint and I had accompanied Mrs. Kennedy to New York on one of her many antiquing visits. While walking down Fifth Avenue one afternoon, we thought she was trying to lose us. I didn't know if it was for real, or if she was just testing us with playful fun and games. It took me back to my earliest formal training as a special agent, when I learned "hound and hare" following techniques. Then it was fun, but now it was serious business.

Looking back, it seems unbelievable that all Clint and I needed to communicate were hand signals while Jacqueline Kennedy ducked in and out of buildings. She never did lose us, as Clint was usually one step ahead of her, anticipating her next move. I can't begin to imagine what the consequences would have been if we had lost her. Thanks to Clint's intuition, we didn't. It turned out to be quite the adrenaline rush for me.

Clint was fabulous to work with. Having been with Mrs. Kennedy from the beginning, he had cultivated a great working relationship with her. He had become familiar with her personality and knew how to diplomatically handle her moods. Mrs. Kennedy trusted him implicitly. This was a huge help to me in making my transition onto the detail, as was the fact that Mrs. Kennedy was familiar with my presence, because I had previously been assigned to her children.

Back in the car, I completed my turn and was now on the Jeff Davis, only a few minutes away from my apartment. If I intended to change my mind, now was the time to do it. Maybe I could get back to the White House in time to withdraw my resignation letter from the outbox before anyone else saw it. Maybe, maybe, but no—I had made up my mind. It was final.

Mrs. Kennedy had managed to keep Clint and me on the move for the previous six months with a whirlwind of activities and travel. Only a week earlier, on Wednesday, April 29, we had been at the 1964 World's Fair in Queens, New York, with Caroline, John Jr., and two of their cousins, Stephen and Jean Kennedy Smith's children Stephen Jr. and William. Stephen Sr. was Mrs. Kennedy's brother-in-law and husband of Jean, one of President Kennedy's younger sisters. The only thing I remember about the World's Fair is the theme song from the Pepsi exhibit, "It's a Small World." I hummed it for days afterward.

The next day, at 3:42 PM, we departed New York City for our return trip to DC. We were flying on the *Caroline*, the Kennedy family's private twin-engine airplane. We arrived in DC at 6:00 PM and headed to the family's new house in the Georgetown neighborhood. Three hours and twenty minutes later we were in a car driving to Atoka, Virginia, where Mrs. Kennedy had her weekend home "Wexford." We arrived at 10:23 PM and I was finally off duty at 11:00 PM with the sounds of "It's a Small World" still ringing in my ears.

I spent the next two days working in Atoka, followed by two more days at the Georgetown residence before I finally got two days off. I was tired, burned out, and ready for a break.

I was still lost in memories when I reached the Crystal House apartments, located at 1900 South Eads Street. I guess I had been driving on autopilot most of the way. It was only midafternoon and most people were still at work, so parking spaces were plentiful. I spotted a space near the walkway leading into my building and pulled in. Reaching back, I grabbed hold of the convertible's

top, pulled it up over my head, and secured it to the front windshield with the two latches. I rolled up the windows and grabbed
a Pan American Airways flight bag that I had placed on the seat
beside me earlier in the day. I pushed down the door locks and
exited my Corvette.

The flight bag I was using that day was only one of several
I had acquired in my travels. In the 1950s and '60s, almost all
airlines passed out flight bags to their passengers. I had flight
bags from Eastern Air Lines (EAL), United Airlines (UAL), Pan
American Airways (Pan Am), and Trans World Airlines (TWA).
These flight bags were a staple item for most special agents on
the White House Detail. They were quite handy, the perfect size
for carrying extra items one might need throughout the day. I
generally used mine to carry my lunch, extra snacks, sunglasses,
and maybe a swimsuit or whatever, depending on where we happened to be going on any particular day. Occasionally I used
my bag to store my handgun, but I always felt uncomfortable
doing so. I had this recurring dream that Mrs. Kennedy would
be rushing out to go somewhere and Clint Hill and I would have
to race after her but I would be unarmed, having left my sidearm
behind. I always woke up with a start and was thankful that it
was only a dream.

The Pan Am bag I was using that day was a favorite that I had
acquired on a stopover in Paris after visiting Greece seven months
earlier. I had other flight bags devoted to specialized purposes: I
used a TWA bag I had acquired on a trip to Italy as a shag bag
for my practice golf balls.

I headed toward my Crystal House apartment building, wondering what my two roommates would think when they heard
what I'd done. Special Agent Dick Johnsen and Special Agent
Dave Grant and I had met when we were assigned to the protection detail guarding President Eisenhower's grandchildren in

Gettysburg, Pennsylvania. All three of us were bachelors at the time, and we were all assigned to the White House Detail after President Kennedy's election. We had shared an apartment ever since. This was our third apartment together in as many years—Dave was the one who always got antsy and wanted a change of scenery. It didn't much matter to me, just as long as I had a place to hang my hat whenever I wasn't traveling.

Dick found our first apartment, which was located at 1850 Columbia Pike in Arlington. It was a great location and an easy commute to work. The management of the building also operated the building next door, and they had regular mixers between the two buildings so we were able to meet other singles. Dick met his future wife at one of these mixers.

Dave, however, got bored with this location and wanted to move. He located a nice apartment on Kensington Parkway in Kensington, Maryland. Our fourth-floor apartment had a balcony overlooking a swimming pool, and we all had visions of bikini-clad sunbathers idling around the pool during the summer months. But the Kensington apartment turned out to be a huge mistake. The commute to the White House took much longer, plus we soon discovered that the three of us were by far the youngest residents. This was not the place for three young Secret Service bachelors on the prowl. Besides, I was hardly ever there, Dick was now in love, and Dave had met a Braniff Airways stewardess of interest. All three of us were anxious to move back to Arlington once our lease expired. So there I was, heading up to my apartment on the eleventh floor of the Crystal House, not knowing what my future would bring.

I entered the building and walked past the lobby desk to the elevators. When the elevator got to my floor, I exited and turned toward my apartment. I went in feeling mentally and emotionally exhausted. I had put myself through a wringer and just wanted to lie down and rest my eyes. I went to the bedroom and dropped my flight bag onto the floor when the telephone rang. I had a feeling I knew who it was.

My senses were right. It was Clint, and he was laughing. "What the hell is this," he asked, "some kind of a joke?"

"It's no joke," I replied. "I'm dead serious. I've made up my mind. That's it. It's final!"

Clint must have arrived at the White House shortly after I had left, because driving home had not actually taken me that long. We talked for a little while, but I don't remember much about our conversation. All I do remember is that I convinced him that my decision was final.

Try as I might, I was unable to put the broken pieces back together. When I was awake, I was fine. There was enough going on to occupy my mind, plus I had to remain alert. But at night after I went to bed, the images from Dallas returned. They were like a videotape loop playing over and over again. Then I started turning positives into negatives. The long hours, the short notices, the change in plans—all the things I once thrived on that made the job interesting and exciting no longer did so. I just couldn't bounce back and move forward. My Secret Service career was drawing to a close.

2

ALL MY EGGS

I WAS TWO YEARS OUT OF COLLEGE, going on twenty-four years old, and still living at home with my parents in Worthington, Ohio. I was uncertain what to do for the rest of my life and under no pressure to move out or move on. I had many fond memories of Worthington and was not ready to make a quick exit. I even remember the day when we moved there.

It was August 1942, right after my seventh birthday, when my parents left Bowling Green, Ohio, and moved to the sleepy little village of Worthington, located in Central Ohio, ten miles due north of Columbus, the state capital. Hoping to ease any anxieties I might have had over the move, Dad let me ride on the front seat of the moving van, sitting in the middle between him and the van's driver. My mother, Evelyn, along with my twelve-year-old sister, Marilyn, and our pet English setter, Windy, followed behind us in the family's black 1939 Plymouth sedan.

My father, Paul Sr., left behind a seventeen-year coaching and teaching career at Bowling Green State University (BG), where he had been an associate professor, head basketball and track coach, assistant football coach, and director of intramural athletics. He also gave up a golfing profession, having been the pro at the Bowling Green Municipal Golf Course.

Years later my father told me that one of his reasons for leaving BG was, of all things, that they were considering recruiting athletes. It was against his philosophy. He strongly believed that you should take the talent you have, teach them the fundamentals, and work from there. (My, how times have changed.) He had accepted a new position with the Ohio Department of Education as the state supervisor of health, physical education, recreation, and safety. It paid $200 more in annual income, a 10 percent raise over his salary at BG.

After our two-vehicle caravan arrived in Worthington, population approximately sixteen hundred, I remained outside exploring the surroundings while everyone else was busy unpacking. A boy showed up on his bicycle and told me his name was Bob. He said he lived just two blocks away, pointing in the direction of his house. He appeared to be about my sister's age and said that he was just curious who was moving into the neighborhood. He was probably really there to check out my sister, and as it turned out, the two of them ended up being classmates starting in the eighth grade.

It didn't take long before our house became a hangout for all the neighborhood kids. We had a vacant lot next door where we played "first bounce or fly" or touch football, depending on the season. Dad had acquired an old wooden backboard from BG before leaving. He first hung it inside our detached two-car garage so we had a place to play basketball, rain or shine. Bob would stop over in the evenings and we kids would play hide-and-seek, and when it really got dark, we all sat around on the front steps of our house and listened to Bob tell scary ghost stories. Growing up in Worthington during the 1940s and 1950s was an age of innocence and adventure for me. Life was good. I was also fortunate to be in a loving home where I never recall hearing a swear word spoken or having anyone ever referred to by anything other than their name.

Eventually the backboard came down from inside the garage and Dad and I put it up outside. Marilyn was now a high school cheerleader, and it gave some members of the basketball team another reason to hang out. Marilyn and Bob never really dated, but they had become best friends, and he always seemed to be around. I never could have imagined in my wildest dreams after first meeting Bob Foster in August 1942 that he would play such an important role in my future.

After graduating from Worthington High School in 1953, I attended Ohio Wesleyan University (OWU), located in Delaware, Ohio, fourteen miles north of Worthington. OWU was far enough away from home that I could have a life of my own, yet close enough for me to hitchhike home on Fridays with my dirty laundry and return to school with clean clothes on Sunday.

Before leaving for OWU, my father told me something very similar to this: "Son, you will find college to be a wonderful experience, and you will learn many new things. However, you will also find that most of your education will come from outside the classroom. You will have an opportunity to meet people from all walks of life, but most of all, you will meet and make many new lifelong friends. These friends will always be there for you, if and when you ever need them. That is more than any textbook can provide."

Ohio Wesleyan had a total enrollment of about twenty-four hundred students. Approximately 95 percent of the student body belonged to either a fraternity or sorority. If you wanted any kind of a social life on campus, you had to join one or the other. The first week at OWU was rush week, when students visited the houses that they were interested in joining and, hopefully, the fraternity or sorority of their choice would invite them to pledge.

Two of my very best friends from high school, Tom Lindblom and Paul Smith, had also chosen to attend OWU. The three of us played golf together on our high school team, and Tom and I were going to be freshman roommates. All of us went through "rush" together but decided not to reveal our choice of fraternity in advance. We would decide on Tuesday night and just show up at the fraternity of our choice.

The three of us were pretty heavily recruited by all the major fraternities. When Tuesday night arrived, all three of us showed up at Sigma Alpha Epsilon to make our pledge. Phi Alpha, everyone!

Four years later I received my bachelor of arts degree with a major in geology. My father had been right. Although I could have put a little more effort into the textbook side of things, I had made many new friends, both on campus and in the SAE house. But now what?

Uncle Sam helped make that decision for me. According to the Selective Service Act of 1948, when a male turned eighteen, he was required by law to register with the local draft board to determine his status for military service. While I was in college, I was classified as "student deferred." As long as I stayed in school, I didn't have to worry about being drafted. But now that I had graduated, I was reclassified as 1-A: "available for service." I knew that if I didn't do something soon, I would be drafted into the army. I did not want that. I wanted to choose which branch of the service to join.

I had heard about the US Navy's Officer Candidate School program. It sounded interesting. "Join the Navy and see the world" was their slogan. The idea appealed to me as adventurous and exciting—and I would be an officer, no less. I applied and passed the necessary exams. Unfortunately, there were no open classes at the time. I was told that I would have to wait for the next opening, whenever that would be.

I couldn't wait. I knew I had to do something soon. My friend Tom Lindblom was in the same situation, so the two of us decided to join the Ohio Air National Guard's 121st Tactical Fighter Wing, located at Lockbourne Air Force Base, just south of Columbus. It was a six-month active duty, a once-a-month meeting, and a two-week summer camp program. "Sleep well tonight. Your National Guard is awake" was their slogan. We were in, and our active duty would not start until fall.

With that settled and a free summer ahead of me, I got on the telephone and called Paul Kirby in Niagara Falls, New York. Paul was a former classmate and fellow geology major. We had talked about taking a camping trip together after graduation to visit all the places we had read about. Paul said he'd get back to me. He called the next day and said, "I'm ready, let's do it, and guess what? My father said we could use the grocery store's Ford panel van." I had not known that Paul's parents were in the grocery business, but this turned out to be a perfect blessing. We would have plenty of room for all our gear, and if we didn't want to set up camp at night, or if it was raining, we could roll out our sleeping bags and sleep inside the truck.

Paul drove down to Worthington to pick me up on the weekend before Independence Day 1957. We loaded my gear into the van along with my sleeping bag and some fishing tackle, just in case the opportunity arose to do some fishing. We intended to take the northern route across the United States starting from Minnesota, the Land of Lakes, and continue west from there, cramming in as many sites as we possibly could.

Monday morning, we were on our way. We drove through Chicago on toward Madison, Wisconsin, heading for Duluth and Hibbing, Minnesota, the first planned stops on our great adventure. Outside of Duluth we were passing one of the many small lakes that Minnesota was famous for, and we decided it would be a beautiful place to stop and settle in for the night. Hibbing could wait. We found a nice spot by the lake's shore, and while Paul started to set up camp, I grabbed my fishing rod and headed off to catch dinner. I didn't even have a chance to get my fishing line wet before I realized that I was fresh mosquito bait. I had never seen so many mosquitoes. I turned around and headed back toward our campsite, slapping and swatting at mosquitoes all the way. When I got there, Paul was slapping and swatting too.

"Let's get the hell out of here," I said, returning my fishing gear to the van. Paul didn't hesitate a moment, and we hurried out of there as fast as we could. Neither one of us had thought to bring along mosquito repellant, but I don't believe it would have made any difference. Those suckers were vicious. We found an empty grocery store parking lot and parked there for the night, sleeping inside the van. We figured we'd be safe and not look too out of place, because the van had KIRBY's MARKET, NIAGARA FALLS, NEW YORK painted on both of its side panels. The following morning, we were up early and continued the last hundred miles or so to Hibbing, where we wanted to see the Hull-Rust Mine, one of the world's largest open-pit iron ore mines. From the observation point where we parked, the view was awesome, but there was no apparent activity. It was July 4, a holiday.

We could see a small shack at the bottom of the open-pit mine, and I said to Paul, "Let's go exploring and get some taconite samples along the way." We grabbed our rucksacks and headed for the bottom, carefully stepping along down the mine's slopes. Apparently we were the only two people in this gigantic hole in the ground that stretched on for miles. It was exciting.

When we reached the shack at the bottom of the mine, we discovered that it was unlocked. There was a hasp but no padlock.

We went in, and I could not believe my eyes. Boxes of TNT, blasting caps, and fuses were stacked in one corner, all of this in an unlocked shack.

"Let's get out of here," I said, suddenly fearing we might get caught and be in real trouble for trespassing. We hurried up the slopes and were on our way without incident. We'd seen enough, and my heart was racing, thinking about what might have been. We were both happy to be back on the road.

We spent two days taking turns driving the next seven hundred miles to Badlands National Park in South Dakota. We were in no hurry. We just wanted to take in as much of the country as we could.

When we arrived at Badlands, we checked in with a park ranger to see about camping overnight, which really wasn't allowed. We explained why we were there, and after he sized us up as being honest and harmless, he made an exception to the rule. He had us follow him in his truck, and he took us to his favorite spot, located on a canyon rim with a great view overlooking the Badlands. He cautioned us about the dangers of hiking in the area and told us how easy it was to get lost, because once you were down in the valleys everything looked the same. He left and said he would be back to check on us later. Paul and I decided to do some exploring, looking for fossilized turtle shells, which were supposed to be abundant and were one of the things that the Badlands were noted for.

Our newfound friend returned later, and the three of us sat around a campfire together enjoying a peaceful evening under the stars. Our ranger friend came back in the morning to see us off and wish us good luck, but he was probably really checking to make sure we cleaned up our campsite.

We left the Badlands and continued west toward the Black Hills of South Dakota. Our next stop was the "Shrine of Democracy,"

Mount Rushmore National Memorial, with its sixty-foot-high heads of four American presidents: George Washington, Thomas Jefferson, Theodore Roosevelt, and Abraham Lincoln. We continued west through the Black Hills to Sheridan, Wyoming, where we spent a few days at a geology field camp that was being taught by Norbert Cygan, a young geology instructor from OWU. Since Paul and I were both geology majors, we had shared some of his classes, which were both interesting and fun. When we had told him about our postgraduation travel plans out West, he told us about the geology field camp he would be teaching in Wyoming that same summer. The camp was sponsored by the University of Wyoming in Laramie, but the actual location was at a ranch near Sheridan, about 250 miles north of Laramie. He suggested that we stop by and see him. Here we were.

We spent three days at the camp, and to pay for our room and board, Paul and I spent mornings helping with chores and cutting and splitting cords of firewood for the winter months ahead. For me, Wyoming was love at first sight. I was ready to go home, pack up my belongings, and move back permanently to become a rancher. But our host and his wife (both graduates of Miami University in Oxford, Ohio) advised me that ranching wasn't all that it appeared to be and Wyoming winters were pretty rough. According to them, I would be much better off pursuing a career in geology. Sometime later, Norb told us that he was taking his students to the Grand Canyon in two weeks, and we agreed to meet again there.

The University of Wyoming had an extension center in Sheridan where Norb had an office. On the morning that we were to leave, Norb was working out of his office, and we needed to borrow his personal car to go pick up our van, which was in for an oil change. He told us to park it on the street when we were finished and to bring the keys back to his office in the Geology Department.

I had purchased a box of fireworks at a local store. Included in the box were a couple of "car bombs," the kind you hook up to a spark plug so that when someone starts the car, they make a loud whistle, create a lot of smoke, and end with a loud bang. They were not really dangerous. They just made a lot of smoke and noise, with no damage to the car or its engine.

I said to Kirby, "Before we return the keys, let's hook up one of my car bombs to Norb's car. He's the kind of guy who could appreciate the joke." Kirby agreed. Two wires extended out of one end of the bombs. I opened the hood of his car and attached one wire to a spark plug and the other to the engine block. I closed the hood, and we headed up to Norb's office to drop off his keys and then be on our way. We thanked Norb, said our good-byes, and told him we would see him at the Grand Canyon in two weeks. The two of us left Sheridan laughing, thinking about Norb's reaction and what he would have to say the next time we saw him.

Now, for the first time since we left home, we had a deadline and a schedule to meet. We headed straight for Yellowstone National Park, Wyoming, then over to Craters of the Moon National Monument, Idaho, and passed through Sun Valley up to Glacier National Park, Montana. From there we went on to Seattle, Washington, and Mount Rainier, which we only got about a thirty-second glimpse of through a break in the clouds. Then we went to Crater Lake, Oregon, and over to Crescent City, California, where we got our first glimpse of the Pacific Ocean. This was a big deal for two guys from the Midwest, so we parked the van along Highway 101 and climbed down a pathway to the shore.

The tide was out and we were able to walk and jump on the rocks, observing real, live starfish, crabs, and other weird marine life. We were running on the beach, frolicking like little kids, when we heard the sound of screeching tires and a loud thump. *Oh my God, the van*, I thought, turning to see what had happened. The van was OK, but I saw a car flying through the air, flipping end over end, with the driver hanging halfway out of the windshield.

Paul and I started running up to the highway, both of us expecting the worst. When we reached the top, we found another car that had apparently been hit by the first car we saw. I ran to the first car, and Paul ran to the second. By the time I got to the first car, the driver had already climbed all the way out of the windshield, and he was sitting by the roadside with no apparent injuries other than some cuts on his chin. I reached into my pocket, took out a handkerchief, and gave it to him to hold over his cuts. I asked if he was OK, and that's when I realized that he was so drunk that he had no idea where he was or what had just happened. I left him sitting there and ran back to see how Paul was doing.

A family of four, two adults and two children, were in the other car, but I don't remember how serious their injuries were. At least nobody had been killed. It took several minutes before another car arrived, and when it did, we asked the driver to go to Crescent City and send for help. We waited quite a while for the police and an ambulance, but once they arrived, Paul and I gave our statements and we were again on our way.

Redwood National Park came next, then the Golden Gate Bridge and San Francisco, then across the Bay Bridge to Oakland, where we spent the night at the house of a female OWU classmate's parents. I got to shower, have a home-cooked meal, and sleep in a real bed for the first time since Paul and I began our trip.

But we couldn't stay to visit. We still had Los Angeles, Hollywood, and San Diego to go in California before heading east to Phoenix, Arizona, and then up to the Grand Canyon to meet back up with Norb Cygan. By now we were taking turns switching between driving and sleeping, not really stopping to visit any one place. We just wanted to be able to say we had been there. We had miles to cover and a commitment to keep.

The hotel/motel/restaurant/bar where everyone was staying was located just outside the entrance to Grand Canyon National Park. We arrived after sunset, right on schedule, and discovered that Norb's crew had eaten dinner and had already taken over the bar. Paul and I joined them at a table, all the while laughing in anticipation of Norb's reaction when he saw the two of us. He spotted us first and was already heading our way when we saw him. We both had huge smiles on our face as he approached, but his face was beet red.

"Uh oh," I said under my breath.

"I'm mad at you guys," he blurted. "You have no idea the trouble and anxiety you caused." He then proceeded to tell us what happened after we left Sheridan.

Later on the same day we left, his wife, Carol, needed to use the family car. She called him at his office, and he told her where we had parked it and to come to his office to pick up his keys, which she did. She located the car, started the engine, and left. Nothing happened. However, after she had parked the car and came back and started it a second time, *BAM, WHISTLE,* and *SMOKE*—tons of it billowed out from under the hood. The bomb, which had misfired the first time, went off, and she went *ballistic.* She called Norb, hysterical and crying. The poor woman thought that she had blown up the family car. By the time Norb got to the scene, the police and fire department were there, and they had already figured out what happened.

Norb was absolutely livid, and I guess I can't blame him. Our little prank had backfired on us, and we had caused undue stress to a friend and his wife. At least the police didn't issue a BOLO ("be on the lookout") for us, which would probably happen in today's world. But did I feel guilty at the time? No, not really. Paul and I could not have choreographed a better outcome, I thought, laughing quietly on the inside. (Norb Cygan's wife, Carol, died from cancer in 1992, so she's not here to accept my apologies, but Norb, if you happen to be reading this, I apologize for any grief we may have caused.)

After spending the next day at the Grand Canyon, we went north into Utah and drove through Glen Canyon, one of the most beautiful and scenic canyons I had ever seen. That was before the Glen Canyon Dam was constructed to form Lake Powell. We took in Zion and Bryce National Parks on the way to Ephraim, Utah, where I had attended a geology field camp the previous summer. We cut across the Wasatch Plateau as we headed for Grand Junction, Colorado, where we again turned south and drove along the Continental Divide, aiming for the oil fields of Oklahoma and then New Orleans.

By now it was early August, and Paul was getting homesick. I wanted to continue on, but we both decided to skip New Orleans and head home, passing through Nashville along the way. By the time we got back to Worthington, I, too, was glad we had cut our trip short. On the journey back, we had resorted to only driving, with no camping or stopping, except to eat in cheap diners. Overall, though, the trip had been a fantastic experience, and we had many good tales to share.

Cowboy Paul Landis, age twenty-two, arrives home from the West, summer 1957. *Author's collection, photo by Paul Kirby*

Paul spent the night in Worthington, and the next morning we said our good-byes. We kept in touch for a while, but that was the last time I ever saw Paul in person. Paul died in 1978, and to this day, I still feel a touch of melancholy whenever I think of him. Together we had seen a lot, learned a lot, and laughed a lot.

I was only home for a few days when my sister, Marilyn, called from Ypsilanti, Michigan. Her husband, Al Fagerstrom, was working on his doctoral degree at the University of Michigan, Ann Arbor. He was a geologist studying paleontology, and he had some fieldwork to finish in order to complete his degree. Al had a particular area in Michigan's Upper Peninsula where he needed to do some additional research. Since I had majored in geology, she wondered if I wanted to go along for the experience.

I enjoyed a week of camping, searching, and chipping away at rock outcrops. Al was super smart, and for that whole week he was in his own paleo paradise. I loved the discovery aspect, but I was beginning to have second thoughts about a career in geology. After we returned to Ypsilanti, I thanked Al for a great week and headed back to Worthington. I knew for certain that paleontology was not my bag—dinosaur bones and volcanoes might be exciting, but not itty-bitty fossils. Fortunately, I didn't have to make a career decision anytime soon.

At the end of the summer, I was due to begin my basic training for the Ohio Air National Guard at Lackland Air Force Base in Texas. The train ride from Union Station in downtown Columbus to San Antonio seemed to go on forever. New recruits joined the train all along the way, and when we finally reached our destination, a bus was waiting to take us to the base to begin our basic training.

I was assigned to a squadron of sixty men, most of whom were college graduates. Our drill instructor was baffled—he didn't know how to react to us. We didn't moan, groan, or complain. He didn't assign us extra push-ups or extra laps around the track because of goof-ups. We just did whatever he asked and helped each other out wherever we could.

I was three weeks into training when I received notice that I had finally been accepted into the US Navy. I was told to report immediately to Newport, Rhode Island, for the beginning of Navy Officer Candidate School, but I declined. I had already made my commitment. Not long after that, I was glad I did. The military was starting to cut back on spending, and my original six months of active duty was reduced to thirteen weeks.

I was home by early December 1957. The Ohio State Buckeyes had won the Big Ten football championship that year, which meant that they would be playing in the New Year's Day Rose Bowl game held in Pasadena, California. Their opponent was to be the University of Oregon, winner of the Pac-12 football conference that year. Three of my friends and I talked about going to the game if we could get tickets. I told them that I would talk to my dad to see what he could do. Woody Hayes, the Ohio State football coach, was a friend of Dad's, so I asked Dad if he would call Woody and ask a favor for us. We ended up with four seats on the fifty-yard line. Now the issue was getting there.

Tom Yates, Frank Slater, and I were all in the Air National Guard. Bill Joseph, a high school classmate, was attending dental school courtesy of the navy. We all had military uniforms and were able to fly for free on any scheduled military flight, as long as space was available. Tom, Frank, and Bill decided on this option, catching a plane from Lockbourne Air Force Base. But I didn't want to travel in uniform. Instead, I decided to hitchhike US Route 40 and US Route 66 on my own. We made hotel reservations in Pasadena, California, and agreed that we would all meet in the hotel bar at 5:00 PM on December 29. My parents were leaving for Florida on Christmas Day, so I figured that was as good a day as any for me to leave too.

Christmas morning was chilly as I walked out the front door of my house. I was wearing my winter topcoat and a dark gray fedora, and I had my suitcase in hand. I walked three and a half blocks to the corner of Evening Street and Ohio Route 161 in Worthington, and I stuck out my thumb. I was dressed nicely to make a good impression as cars passed by. I did not want people to think I was a bum. I was only standing there for about ten minutes when I hitched my first ride.

"Where ya headed?" the driver asked.

"Pasadena," I replied. "California!"

"I'm not going to California," he said, "but I can get you as far as St. Louis, Missouri. Hop on in."

I could hardly believe my luck. My first ride would take me all the way to St. Louis, about four hundred miles. The driver turned out to be quite friendly and chatty, and the next nine hours flew by quickly. By the time we reached East St. Louis, it was dark. My driver had reached his destination, so I asked him to drop me off at an AAA-rated motel somewhere close to US Route 40.

On my second day, I wasn't quite so lucky. I had my thumb out before 7:00 AM, but all the cars just drove by without slowing down. Everyone seemed to be in a hurry. After about three hours of this nonsense, I decided that if I wanted to make any headway, I needed to break down and catch a local crosstown bus. The bus wasn't very fast and made quite a few stops along the way, but at least I was moving. Three hours later I reached the junction of Route 40 and Route 66. It had taken me six hours to get to the start of the famous historic highway.

Three more rides covered the five hundred miles to Oklahoma City. This is where my luck came through again. I caught one ride that took me the next thousand miles, almost twenty hours of driving.

This driver was a talker, a real BSer. He had something to do with a logging camp in northern Arizona and wanted to hire me to work there. I guess he thought I was down on my luck and needed a job. He told me that the pay was good and that most of the men got along "real good" most of the time and only got in fights "once in a while" but got over it "real quick." The lumberjacking part sounded intriguing, but fistfighting for entertainment wasn't really my calling. Anyway, that's where he was headed. We traveled through Amarillo, Texas, and Tucumcari, Albuquerque, and Gallup, New Mexico. We were now in Arizona desert country, and when we reached Arizona Route 87, he said that he had to exit there and head north. We said our good-byes and wished each other luck.

It was around midnight as the lights of his pickup truck faded to the north. There were no intersection lights here, so it quickly became dark, and I mean *dark*. At this point Route 66 was just a flat and straight two-lane highway that stretched for miles in each direction. The only light came from the headlights of cars and trucks as they flew by. If there was a speed limit, it was ignored. The cars were going so fast the drivers probably couldn't even see me soon enough to stop. It didn't take me long to realize that my efforts to catch a ride at this location, at this hour of night, were not only futile but also dangerous.

The only sign of civilization was a nearby "trading post." I started trudging toward it while pondering what to do next. I saw gas pumps and thought maybe I could get permission to hang around and hitch a ride from someone when they stopped for gas. *Good idea, Paul*, I thought. As I got closer, I started having this funny feeling. Things were looking familiar. Suddenly I remembered: I had been here before. It was the Jack Rabbit Trading Post. I had come here with my parents in August 1948 when I was twelve years old. My sister had worked a summer job at a dude ranch near Boulder, Colorado, and we were on our way to pick her up. I especially remembered the trading post because of the way it advertised. For hundreds of miles, there would be an occasional sign cut in the shape of a jackrabbit and printed only with a mileage number. As you traveled along and got closer and closer, the numbers got smaller, and of course your curiosity grew and grew. By the time you finally reached this destination, your curiosity was piqued, and you just had to stop to see what it was all about. What a simple and great way to advertise, I thought, and what a small world. How could I end up in the middle of nowhere and that nowhere is somewhere I had been before? Wild!

I entered the Jack Rabbit, told the cashier working there my story, and was granted permission to try hitching a ride outside by the pumps.

The Jack Rabbit Trading Post was a combination gas station, souvenir shop, and diner. It was the only sign of civilization for miles in every direction. After thinking about it, it was an ideal location. It was an oasis in the desert. It was the perfect spot for the traveler in need of fuel or food. I went outside and sat on a bench next to a wooden cigar-store Indian, waiting for my stagecoach to arrive. I waited and I waited. After an eternity of no activity other than my stomach rumbling, I decided to go inside and get something to eat.

The diner was deserted, except for one patron sitting alone at the counter. I put my suitcase on the floor next to a round chrome stool cushioned with dark green Naugahyde and sat down, placing my topcoat and fedora on another seat that separated the two of us. I spotted a lone piece of apple pie in a glass pastry case behind the counter. It looked pretty good, and my stomach rumbled louder.

"I'll take that last piece of apple pie and a hot cup of coffee," I said to the short-order cook when she emerged from the kitchen. "A hamburger too."

While I waited for my burger to arrive, I started to chat with the man next to me. One topic led to another, and before long I was listening to his lament, a real down-and-out story. He went on and on about how he lost his job, his wife left him, and he had no money. He was trying to get to San Francisco by way of Palm Springs to pick up money from a friend who "owed him." His car was outside in the parking lot, but the problem was that it was out of gas. He had been washing dishes here at the Jack Rabbit to earn enough to move on, but they had just laid him off, and he didn't know what he was going to do next.

I ate and listened, patiently waiting for the *Can you loan me some money?* question, but it never came. I knew I wasn't about to give him any money anyway, no matter how sad his tale of woe, but I was also feeling really sorry for him. He seemed nice enough, like he just happened to be down on his luck.

When he first mentioned that his car was out of gas, I had an idea, but I waited to hear him out. When he didn't ask me for money I said, "Tell you what, I'm supposed to be at a friend's house in Colton, California, on December 28, tomorrow. I'll fill your car with gas if you'll drive me to Colton. We can go through Palm Springs on the way." I knew Palm Springs was out of the way for me, but what the heck. What were a few more miles and hours when I had a guaranteed ride the rest of my way, knowing I would be on schedule?

His eyes started to get a little watery when we shook hands to seal the deal. As we left the diner, I was feeling exhilarated, and I could tell he must have felt the same by the way he walked and the tone of his voice. We filled his car with gas, and moments later it was so long, Jack Rabbit.

We headed west, and after reaching Flagstaff it was south down through Oak Creek Canyon toward Phoenix, and then west again on Route 10 to Palm Springs. We alternated between driving and sleeping, and I was the one sleeping when we reached Palm Springs. After the man conducted his business, we were off on the last leg of our trip together. When we reached Colton, I filled his gas tank for one last time. He dropped me off at my friend's house, and then left for his new life in San Francisco. I felt sad for him and hoped everything worked out for the better here in the Golden State.

My Colton friend was a saint. We had only known each other for the few weeks we spent together in basic training at Lackland AFB, but he and his parents welcomed me with open arms. I spent the night (sleeping in a bed), and the next afternoon my friend drove me the final sixty miles to Pasadena, dropping me off at my hotel.

I walked into the hotel lobby on December 29 at 5:15 PM. I was fifteen minutes late. *Not bad*, I thought, *for winging it over the last two-thousand-plus miles.* I spotted a post in the middle of the hotel lobby and dropped my suitcase beside it with my topcoat and hat on top. I saw a lounge/bar sign and immediately headed that way. When I stepped through the door, a loud cheer came from a booth across the room. My three friends were already there, just like we planned. I headed across the room to join them. Let the party begin, and party we did—*all night long.*

We spent the entire night carousing, visiting various night-spots in Hollywood and Pasadena, relying on taxi drivers for suggestions. We finally returned to the hotel sometime after dawn the following morning. My suitcase, topcoat, and hat were still in the exact spot where I had left them over twelve hours earlier. I grabbed my things, and we all headed to our room to catch up on some much-needed sleep.

There were lots of Ohio State football fans and students staying in our hotel, so we had no problem locating parties to attend, and that's what the four of us did until New Year's Day. I had completely forgotten about the three-hour time difference between Ohio and California, so when we started talking about attending the Rose Parade on New Year's Day, it meant a wake-up call for me—and an early one at that. Every year in Ohio the parade started on television at 10:00 AM, but that was of course just 7:00 AM in Pasadena. We were told that in order to get a good spot along the parade route we should be there at least two hours early. People even slept out overnight in order to have a good spot. Adding an additional hour to get there from the hotel meant that I was up and out of the hotel by 4:00 AM.

Bill Joseph and I were the only two who actually made it to the parade, while Tom and Frank slept in. The parade was spectacular to view in person, and I am happy I took the time to attend.

Afterward, the four of us reunited at the hotel and headed to the Rose Bowl, where Ohio State defeated the University of Oregon by a score of 10 to 7.

I don't remember celebrating much that night. I think the four of us were pretty much partied out, and besides, we had to think about heading home the next day. Frank had decided to hitchhike home with me, while Bill and Tom had a military hop to catch. Frank and I both wanted to go to Las Vegas to see the Strip—the long row of casinos that stretched four miles out from downtown. Because of the travel time and logistics involved, we decided to let a Greyhound bus take us those first 280 miles. We would arrive in the late afternoon and could then resume thumbing our way home the next day.

We arrived in Las Vegas as planned; however, our suitcases did not. They had mistakenly been placed on a bus going to Salt Lake City, Utah, some 430 miles to the north. Even if they were caught in time, there was no possible way to get them back sooner than the following morning. Like it or not, the two of us were stuck in Vegas for an extra day. Neither one of us had any gambling money, but we decided to walk the Strip anyway. The sky was filled with light from a beautiful sunset while the glittering lights of Vegas began to cast their spell.

Soon enough we felt the pull of the Golden Nugget casino. We had both heard of it and seen pictures, and this was our chance to see the real thing. "Let's go," I said to Frank, and we headed that way. From there we headed to the Silver Slipper, another casino we had seen in the movies. We went from casino to casino all night long, ending up at the Dunes, the last casino on the Strip at that time.

I had no idea how to play craps. I was watching one of the tables at the Dunes when the stickman shoved the dice in front of me. I shook my head no to pass, but a gentleman standing next to me said, "Go ahead, roll the dice," and he placed a silver dollar down in front of me. I rolled the dice. Then I rolled them again, and again, and again. Everyone at the table kept placing bets as I continued to roll. I have no idea how many times I rolled the dice, but people kept betting and winning money. The dice were finally placed in front of the man who had urged me to roll them in the first place. I have no idea how much money he won, but it was a lot. He gave me a silver dollar for my efforts.

Frank and I started to leave, and as we passed an empty lounge, we heard piano music and singing coming from inside. We decided to investigate. To our surprise, Nat King Cole was the one playing the piano, and he was singing along with Lena Horne. He nodded his head, inviting us over, and we joined them and a couple of other stragglers for an early morning singalong. What a great way to end our night on the town and to begin our new day.

When we left the Dunes, the light of dawn was beginning to brighten the sky. We had walked the entire length of the four-mile Strip. Frank and I had been to the Golden Nugget, the Silver Slipper, the Flamingo, the Desert Inn, the Sands, the Riviera, the Tropicana, and the Dunes—a total of eight casinos.

It was midmorning by the time we walked back downtown and were able to retrieve our bags from the Greyhound bus terminal. Thank goodness, because we were both exhausted and needed some shut-eye. We found a place to stay near the terminal—a real fleabag hotel, but we didn't care. All we wanted to do was sleep. Frank got a ten-dollar single room with a single bed. I cost a buck extra. We pulled the mattress off of the bedsprings and onto the floor. It wasn't the best arrangement—there was no room to walk or move without stepping over something—but we each had our own bed. We flipped the silver dollar that I had received earlier to see who got the mattress. I won the toss, and the next thing I knew, I was out like a light.

The next morning, we again decided to take a bus, this time to Hoover Dam, which was only about thirty miles from Las Vegas, less than an hour's bus ride.

We spent some time touring and then walked across the dam to the east side, where US Route 93 continued on to Kingman, Arizona, and connected to Route 66 heading east. I was wondering how well the two of us would do hitchhiking together. Expecting a driver to have room for one extra person was one thing, but for two, I didn't know. Regardless, we were in this together, and I was happy to have a friend to travel with.

Surprisingly, I didn't have to wait long for my answer. A car passed us, and suddenly its brake lights came on. As it slowed to a stop a few yards ahead of us, Frank and I grabbed our bags and started running toward it. The driver had all the car windows open, so when we reached it, he asked us, "How far are you guys going?" We answered, "Columbus, Ohio," in unison. He replied, "Well, I'm going to Ohio too—to Akron, Ohio."

Frank and I looked at each other in disbelief. Could this be true, I wondered? I mean, how lucky could we get? He would have to pass through Columbus on his way. "Only thing is," he said, interrupting my thoughts, "I want to take my time and sightsee along the way. I'm originally from Italy. I work in Akron and stay with a relative who lives there. I promised myself that if and when I came to America, I would see as much of the United States as I could. That's what I'm doing, and I'm on my way back home. If you two want to join me, it's OK with me, but that's what I'm doing. I'll even drop you off at your homes if you want."

His offer was a real no-brainer. I had no deadlines to meet, and neither did Frank. We put our things in the trunk of his car, and we were on our way.

The three of us spent our first night together sleeping outdoors around a campfire at the south rim of the Grand Canyon. This was my second visit to the Grand Canyon within the past seven months, and my fifth visit overall. It was a first for Frank, and of course, a first for our new friend. We spent the next seven days working our way back to Ohio, stopping wherever our ride home desired.

Frank lived in Linworth, Ohio, a small town about two miles west of Worthington. In the midmorning of January 12, 1958, we arrived at Frank's house and dropped him off. A few minutes later we were on West North Street in Worthington. My father happened to be in the front yard of our one-and-a-half-story, gray asbestos-shingle Cape Cod when we stopped at the end of our driveway. I introduced him to the person who had driven us all the way home from Nevada, before my friend of eleven days left to continue on his way home to Akron. I had been gone for eighteen days and had not called home once. It never occurred to me that my parents might be worried.

As Dad and I walked up the driveway to the house, he quietly reprimanded me for my thoughtlessness. "Don't you ever do that to your mother again," he said. "She has been worried sick." I apologized, and that was that.

Now that I was home, playtime was over. It was time to get serious about a full-time job, a career. I mailed a few résumés to some major oil companies hoping to get lucky and land a job in oil exploration, but my heart wasn't in it. I knew that I would have to go back to school for a master's degree, and that would be a waste of my time. I was not ready to become a serious student. I was having too much fun enjoying my freedom. I loved hunting, fishing, and outdoor activities. I thought about being a park ranger, and my father introduced me to the head of the Ohio Department of Natural Resources, but he did more to discourage me than anything else. I really didn't understand why he'd do that, and that kind of burst my bubble.

Paul Landis Jr., age twenty-three, with father
Paul Landis Sr. at Medina, Ohio, game
preserve, fall 1958. *Author's collection*

I was working part-time at Wilson's Men's Wear, a clothing
store located in Graceland shopping center near Worthington. It
wasn't like I was living at home and doing nothing. I earned enough
to cover the few expenses I had, plus I liked the hours, 12:00–
9:00 PM. That allowed me to get up at dawn, play a round of golf,
and clean up before reporting for work at noon. I usually met my
buddies for a beer or two after work, and then went through the
same routine the next day. I was having a great summer with no
real responsibilities and playing the best golf in my life. Plus I was
not getting any pressure from my parents to move out and move on.

I was also starting to fantasize about a possible future in golf.
I lacked the confidence to play professionally, but my favorite

aunt owned a par 3 golf course that I wanted to manage and possibly upgrade with night lighting. But too many family issues scratched that idea. Besides, I learned that her property was going to be taken over by eminent domain for an interstate highway intersection in the near future. Oh well, at least I still had my job at Wilson's Men's Wear.

It was sometime toward the end of that summer when the possibility of becoming a Secret Service agent first entered my mind. Bob Foster, my sister's friend from high school, had joined the Secret Service in July 1956. After spending his first six months working out of the Columbus Field Office, Bob was transferred to Fort Belvoir in Virginia for additional training, and then on to the White House Detail, guarding President Dwight D. Eisenhower. He was married in May 1957, and he and his wife, Peggy, lived in an apartment in Arlington, Virginia. Bob occasionally came back home to Worthington to see his parents, and I usually had the opportunity to see him during these visits.

It was on one of these chance visits, over Labor Day weekend 1958, that my interest in the Secret Service was triggered. Bob was a great storyteller, and he talked about his Secret Service experiences with much enthusiasm. The more he talked, the more interested I became. I began thinking that being able to protect the president of the United States had to be the coolest job in the universe. *I want to do that.* I knew the Secret Service protected the president and also investigated counterfeiting, but I had absolutely no idea what else they did or what qualifications were required to become a special agent.

Bob left town before I had a chance to really question him about his work, so I called his wife, Peggy, asking her to have him send me more information. I soon received a letter from Bob dated September 7 in which he talked about the long days on protection and the low pay. As far as the investigation aspect

was concerned, there was a lot of report writing, and being able
to type was a big asset. All in all, it was "very rewarding," if you
liked this kind of work. He suggested I call Arvid Dahlquist, special agent in charge (SAIC) of the Columbus Field Office.

I met with SAIC Dahlquist the following week. At the con-
clusion of our first interview, he told me to go home and think
about everything we'd discussed for a week and to call him back
if I was still interested.

I didn't need a week. I knew then and there that this was
for me, but I followed his instructions. Exactly one week later, I
picked up the telephone and called.

I next received a letter dated October 3, 1958, from the US
Department of the Treasury. From its founding in 1865 until
it became part of the newly established Department of Home-
land Security in 2003, the Secret Service was part of the Treasury
Department. Their letter advised me to call "as soon as possible to
arrange an appointment to take a written examination for Treasury Enforcement Agent. Upon completion of the mental examination, you will be referred to a Federally designated doctor for
a physical examination. This physical examination, as explained
during your original interview, will be at your expense."

Over the next month, I received other letters from the Treasury
Department. The next one, dated October 13, was instructions
for me to hand the letter to an examining physician to determine
my physical health.

My biggest worry up to that point had been meeting the min-
imum height requirement of five foot eight. During my exam, I
stretched and stretched as much as I possibly could without standing on my tiptoes. If I had been a rubber band stretched to its
limit and snapped, I would have flown across the room. Later
that same month, on October 24, I received notice that I had
passed both the mental and physical exams required to become

REFER TO FILE NO.   2-4-210.0

TREASURY DEPARTMENT
UNITED STATES SECRET SERVICE
FIELD FORCE

OFFICE   2-4
ADDRESS: P. O. LOCK BOX NO. 2056

Columbus 16, Ohio,
October 13, 1958.

TO THE EXAMINING PHYSICIAN:

Dear Sir:

The bearer, Paul E. Landis, Jr., whose address is 111 West North Street,
Worthington, Ohio, is being considered for an agent's position in the
U. S. Secret Service.

The duties of these positions are very arduous and personnel engaged on
such duties must be in excellent physical and mental condition. They
must:

     (a)   Be able to work irregular hours, day or night, and
           in all sorts of weather and for prolonged periods.

     (b)   Be able to walk or run rapidly for long distances,
           often in very hot weather.

     (c)   Be fit to operate automobiles, various types of
           weapons, and other equipment.

     (d)   Have steady nerves, good eyesight, good physical
           strength, the use of both feet, both hands (includ-
           ing all fingers) and be alert mentally.

These physical qualifications are necessary not only for ability to perform the strenuous duties but, on occasion, an agent's own life and the
lives of others may depend upon his fitness to act in emergency situations.

Will you please give this applicant a thorough physical examination, being
sure to execute all sections of the enclosed examination form. Any com-
ments you desire to make under the heading "Remarks" will be appreciated.
Please forward your report direct to me using the enclosed self-addressed
envelope. Your fees, if any, for this examination should be collected
from the applicant.

                          Very truly yours,

                          Arvid J. Dahlquist

                          Arvid J. Dahlquist,
                          Special Agent in Charge.

Enclosures - 2

Author's collection

a special agent. Having been a little squirt growing up, I now felt like I was ten feet tall—but I still had to pass a background check.

I hadn't really put much thought into my background investigation. Now all sorts of what-ifs started to enter my mind. How would *they*, whatever *they* were, affect the results of my background check? What about all the hours I'd spent sitting inside the principal's office at school; or the BB gun that little Susie Bonnell, who lived next door, wanted to see, the one that her mother wanted to wrap around my neck; or the stink bomb that I hid in the radiator in my high school English class? What about the time I was arrested for drag racing in my father's 1950 Ford sedan? I loved fireworks and had made all sorts of bombs and stuff, not to destroy anything, just for fun and for the bang. What about the car bomb misfire in Wyoming?

Only my parents and a few close friends knew that I had applied for a position with the Secret Service, so when neighbors, former teachers, and fraternity brothers from Ohio Wesleyan started calling about two men poking around and asking questions about me, I realized it was raising concerns around town. Remember, we lived in a small community, and word spread fast. I managed to brush off most of the inquiries as no big deal, but the months seemed to roll on, and on, and on.

One evening during this long, drawn-out waiting process, Dad sat down with me. He said, "Son, it's been a while and you have all your eggs in one basket. Don't you think that you should start looking around for something else?"

"Dad," I replied, "this is what I really want to do. I'm going to get this job. I just know it. I can feel it."

Nothing else appealed to me, and I wasn't about to think about what to do if I failed my background check. I was a Secret Service agent. It was like Earl Nightingale said on *The Strangest Secret*, a motivational album that had recently become a bestseller: "We become what we think about."

Finally, on Wednesday, July 1, 1959, the letter arrived. It was dated two days earlier.

TREASURY DEPARTMENT
UNITED STATES SECRET SERVICE
FIELD FORCE

OFFICE Columbus 16, Ohio
ADDRESS: P. O. LOCK BOX NO. 2056

June 29, 1959

Mr. Paul E. Landis, Jr.,
111 West North Street,
Worthington, Ohio.

Dear Mr. Landis:

Confirming my telephone call to you, this date, please
be advised that Chief U. E. Baughman, has requested me
to inform you that you have been selected for appointment to the position of Special Agent, grade GS-7,
$4980. per annum, in the Cincinnati, Ohio, office, ef-
fective October 5, 1959.

You should arrange your personal affairs so you can
report to the Cincinnati office on the morning of October
5, 1959. You will report to SAIC Gerard B. McCann, Room
737, Federal Building, Fifth & Walnut Streets, Cincinnati,
Ohio, at your own expense.

Very truly yours,

Arvid J. Dahlquist,
Special Agent in Charge.

3

THE QUEEN CITY

PAYCOR STADIUM IS AN OUTDOOR FOOTBALL STADIUM located on the banks of the Ohio River in downtown Cincinnati. Formerly Paul Brown Stadium, it opened in August 2000 and is the current home of the Cincinnati Bengals. In 1959, however, this same location was nothing but a parking lot paved with blocks of brownish-gray and black granite that angled down into the Ohio River. There were no barriers at the bottom, so in theory you could drive straight down and into the river itself. It was challenging enough to park there on a good weather day, but as I later learned, when it rained or snowed the pavers became quite slippery and it was a real challenge to avoid slipping and sliding down the bank into the river. Also, for obvious reasons, I had to make sure I parked high enough when the river was rising. My first visit was a little scary, but the fact that several other cars were already parked there was reassuring. Even better, it was free and located only a few short blocks from the United States Post Office and Courthouse building, where the US Secret Service field office was located. The lot is where I parked my black 1959 MGA on the morning of October 5, 1959. I walked up the sloping riverbank to level ground and headed toward the nine-story courthouse building at the northeast corner of Walnut and Fifth Streets. I was nervous, but it was a beautiful sunny day, which helped ease my anxieties.

When I reached the courthouse, I noticed that everyone was using a street-level side entrance and not the imposing front steps. I followed the crowd into the building, and a guard directed me to the elevator that took me to the floor where the Secret Service office was located. I exited the elevator and walked down the hallway searching for room numbers. My echoing footsteps were all that I heard, even though there were other people on the same floor headed to work. I finally reached an opaque glass door with gold embossed letters outlined in black that said, UNITED STATES SECRET SERVICE.

Here I go, I thought as I took a deep breath, turned the brass knob, and stepped through the doorway into my future.

The first person to greet me was SAIC Gerard McCann. He was about six feet tall, medium build, with neatly trimmed, thinning gray hair and a bald spot on top of his head. He was wearing a gray sharkskin suit and carried himself with an air of friendly authority. I received a warm welcome and felt immediately at ease. We chitchatted while I was given a brief tour of the offices, and then I was introduced to Edith Jones, the office secretary. I am guessing Miss Jones was in her late fifties. She was petite, had short, wavy gray hair, and wore wire-rimmed glasses. She had a warm, friendly smile, and we immediately connected. I knew that I would be depending on her a lot.

I was then introduced to Special Agent John "Jack" Taylor, and SAIC McCann said, "Come join us, Jack. We're going across the street for a cup of coffee."

I thought to myself, *Wait a minute, I haven't even been on the job for fifteen minutes and already we're taking a coffee break, and on government time at that. What gives?* I was about to receive my first on-the-job training (OJT) lesson in public relations.

The three of us rode the elevator down to the first floor of the courthouse building. Across the street we entered a café. It was jammed with law enforcement personnel of all kinds. Sitting in a booth on that first day drinking coffee, I met the postal inspector, the heads of all the local treasury departments, police detectives, even the police chief of Cincinnati. Everyone was exchanging war stories and filling each other in on the events of the past weekend. We learned who had been arrested and put in jail and who had been released. It was an information exchange. We spent maybe twenty or thirty minutes there and then headed back up to our office.

On the way back, SAIC McCann said, "Paul, Headquarters may not approve, and they don't need to know, but you can't put a price tag on that first half hour of each week. Those people you met are our friends. If they know we are looking for someone and they come across them or already have them in custody, they will call us. It can save hours of legwork trying to track them down. That in itself is priceless. It cuts both ways too. If we have someone in custody, we let them know."

I got the point, and over the following weeks it proved to be rewarding on more than one occasion. Some things just can't be taught in a classroom, and here I thought we were just heading out for a cup of coffee and a Danish.

After we returned to the office, SAIC McCann assigned me to a desk and gave me a little green 3½-by-6-inch memorandum book. He told me to use it to keep track of my daily activities. Every agent had to carry one. It was to be used for reference purposes when I typed my daily report, which I had to do first thing every morning. He then gave me the Secret Service Manual, approximately seven hundred 8½-by-11-inch typewritten pages. My assignment: start reading, which I did for the rest of the morning. After a lunch break, SAIC McCann took me out for a driving test, during which I had to perform several maneuvers just to be sure I could be entrusted with a government vehicle. We returned to the office for the second time that day, and I spent the rest of the afternoon getting oriented on office procedures.

Day two was a little more interesting. I typed my daily report and spent the morning reading the Secret Service Manual. After lunch, SAIC McCann took me to the firing range located in the basement of our building. Our office had a .22 caliber version of a Colt Police Special revolver that was used to practice marksmanship. The reason we used .22 caliber ammunition for practice was because it was much cheaper than .38 caliber ammo. Headquarters only issued one box of fifty .38 caliber shells per agent every three months for practice, hardly enough to become and remain proficient with a handgun. We spent an hour and a half reviewing slow, timed, and rapid firing using only a single-handed grip. No such thing as a two-handed grip existed at that time, and all practice was from a standing position only. If I wanted to be on protection, I would have to be able to score and maintain an "expert" rating of 270 out of 300, with both right and left hands.

No sooner had SAIC McCann and I returned to the office when SA Taylor came up to me and said, "Come on, Paul. Grab your coat. You and I are going to Dayton, Ohio. I have to do some interviews on a check-forgery case." With less than two full days on the job, I was heading out into the field—no commission book (official identification), no weapon, and definitely no experience.

We spent the rest of the day and evening interviewing check payees and possible suspects. SA Taylor conducted the interviews, and I observed. We wrapped up the interviews at 10:30 PM and headed back to Cincinnati, finishing our day at midnight. It had been a long but great day for me. I was having fun, and quickly learning that the Secret Service was not a regular nine-to-five job.

From that day on, SA Taylor took me under his wing. He was right out of central casting, with the perfect Hollywood looks of a special agent, especially when he wore his fedora. He reminded me of all the characters I had grown up listening to in *The FBI in Peace and War* on the radio and seeing in black-and-white movies and early television shows like *Treasury Men in Action*. He also reminded me of Alan Ladd, a popular movie star of the 1940s. Best of all, he was a great teacher and mentor, and I learned most of my investigative skills from him during my Cincinnati assignment.

When I first learned I was going to be working and living in Cincinnati, I purchased a copy of the *Cincinnati Enquirer* and found a room for rent in the classified section. Mrs. Blankenbuehler, a recently widowed grandmother, was offering a room in her home for five dollars per week. I checked it out and it was perfect. I was on my own as far as board was concerned, but I did have use of the kitchen, the refrigerator, and utensils for preparing my own meals. It was an ideal arrangement, because it allowed me the freedom to come and go as I pleased.

When I got up on the morning of day three, I didn't know it yet, but I was already in big trouble with my landlady. By the time I came downstairs, Mrs. B had already prepared a pot of coffee and was fixing her breakfast. I greeted her with a cheery "Good morning," but she did not seem cheery and did not reply. I let it go, fixed a glass of juice and bowl of cereal, and joined her at the kitchen table. I tried some small talk, but she wasn't talking.

Finally, out of the blue, she blurted, "Where were you last night?"

"What?" I replied.

"Where were you?" she said again, adding, "Why did you come in so late?"

Thinking that it was really none of her business but biting my tongue, I replied, "I was working. I had to go to Dayton, Ohio, with another agent who was on an investigation. What's the problem?"

It turned out that being the kind and thoughtful person she was, she had gone out of her way to prepare a special surprise dinner for me, and I was a no-show. I did my best to apologize and explain that even though my job had regular assigned hours, it didn't mean I could always leave work when I wanted. My regular hours were 8:30 AM to 5:30 PM, but they were not written in stone. Sometimes I would have to work late. I also reminded her that even though I appreciated her thoughtfulness and generosity, my meals were not a part of our agreement.

By the time I left for work, Mrs. B was feeling much better, but from that day on, that sweet, dear lady always fixed enough dinner for two, "just in case." If I didn't make it, she at least had the next day's lunch already prepared. From then on there were no more issues over meals, and more often than not, we ate dinner together—and I wasn't about to complain.

After arriving at work on day three, I typed my daily report and did some reading, and SAIC McCann issued me a pair of handcuffs and my own official handgun, a .38 caliber, six-shot Colt Police Special revolver with a four-inch barrel. I still had to use the .22 caliber office revolver on the firing range, but I could practice as much as I wanted as long as a range officer was on duty. I was on the job for less than a week and my daily routine was already established for the rest of my first month: read, practice on the pistol range, accompany SA Taylor on investigations, and observe everything.

My first three months in Cincinnati were probationary, which meant that every thirty days, SAIC McCann submitted an evaluation report to Headquarters in Washington, DC, regarding my progress. After the initial three months, I would have to wait an additional three months before I could be assigned to a temporary thirty-day protection assignment. No formal training was scheduled at that time.

The three main functions of the Secret Service in 1959–60 were presidential protection, suppression of counterfeiting, and suppression of forgery. Forgery work mainly consisted of investigating stolen Social Security checks, which at the time were delivered by mail on the first Monday of the month. (Direct deposits of Social Security checks were not widely available until the 1970s.) Gangs of check thieves, who knew when the Social Security checks were being mailed out, would be on the lookout and grab them from mailboxes as soon as they were delivered. These stolen checks formed the majority of all cases in Cincinnati. Counterfeiting was mostly limited to larger cities like New York, Los Angeles, and Chicago.

I was eventually assigned cases of my own, and I loved investigating and chasing down leads. SAIC McCann gave me a pile of what he called "dead cases" that he wanted closed out, and he got upset with me because I would keep the cases open to follow up on leads. He finally told me, "Paul, you don't understand. I want these cases closed. They are not worth pursuing. Our office gets graded on the number of cases we close, not on the number we have open or pending."

I did manage to close a few cases in the next three months, but I only had one arrest and one court appearance on my own before the end of my first six months of on-the-job training. On March 27, 1960, I left Cincinnati for my "temporary" assignment. I was to be part of the team responsible for the protection of President Eisenhower's four grandchildren, who lived in Gettysburg, Pennsylvania, but I was required to check in at Secret Service Headquarters in Washington, DC, first.

4

GETTYSBURG AND
PROTECTION

M Y FIRST DAY on temporary protection began at 9:00 AM on
Monday, March 28, 1960, in Washington, DC. I reported
to Secret Service Headquarters located in the Treasury Building at
1500 Pennsylvania Avenue NW, right next to the White House.
I was greeted by SAIC James M. Beary, who fifteen minutes later
took me to meet Chief U. E. Baughman, head of the Secret Service,
the man who had hired me but whom I had never met in person.

Needless to say, I was a little nervous anticipating my first face-
to-face meeting with the chief. After my introduction, SAIC Beary
left, and it seemed that the chief had no sooner put me at ease
than SAIC Beary returned and put an end to our brief meeting.
I was beginning to sense how things were run in Washington
when we arrived at our next destination.

We were in the basement of the Treasury Building, where
the US Coast Guard, then a sister agency within the Treasury
Department, operated an indoor pistol range. It was time to test
my marksmanship skills. I had to shoot five rounds each of slow
fire, timed fire, and rapid fire at a stationary bull's-eye target with
my right hand and then my left hand.

49

I don't remember my score, but I passed and was sent across East Executive Avenue to the White House, where I met Assistant to the Special Agent in Charge (ATSAIC) Stu Stout, who gave me written directions to Gettysburg. SA Ken Iacovoni joined me, and at 1:00 PM the two of us left Washington, DC, in my MGA for the two-hour drive to Gettysburg. After arriving and checking into our assigned motel, I had just enough time to shed my suit and tie for a sport shirt, slacks, and sport coat and head to work. I was scheduled to work the 4:00 PM to midnight shift. Ken didn't have to report to work until the midnight shift.

Major John Eisenhower's residence was located near the outskirts of town, on a corner plot next to the 189-acre farm of his father, President Dwight D. Eisenhower. When I came tooling up the gravel driveway in my MGA, there was only one person there to greet me, ATSAIC William "Bill" Barton. ATSAIC Barton was in the process of explaining to me how things operated when David Eisenhower, age eleven, popped out the side door of the house and said he wanted to go over to Granddad's house. I happened to be the only available agent, since all the others were out with the other three Eisenhower grandchildren (Barbara Anne, age ten; Susan, age eight; and Mary Jean, age four).

ATSAIC Barton turned to me and said, "Paul, why don't you take David over to the president's farmhouse. You can take that station wagon over there, and don't worry, David can show you the way."

What? Don't worry? I hadn't been on the job for ten minutes, I had no idea what I was doing, and already I was in charge of protecting this kid's life. *What do you mean don't worry?* I thought. "OK," I hesitantly replied as David entered the front passenger side of the station wagon while I slid in behind the steering wheel and closed the door.

As I pulled out of the driveway, the conversation went something like this. "Hi, I'm David," David said in a friendly, polite voice.

"I know," I replied. "I'm Mr. Landis."

"Hi, Mr. Landis, nice to meet you. Just follow this road for a little way, and I'll tell you where to turn."

As we were driving along, I was lost in thought, not knowing what to expect. I didn't even know what I was supposed to be doing other than driving. Should I be watching out for kidnappers? Roadblocks? What?

I was a little nervous when David said, "You're new at this, aren't you?"

Not wanting to appear too surprised, I replied with a casual, "Why, what makes you think that?"

"Because you didn't call in on the radio," he replied. "You are supposed to call my location using the dashboard radio." The station wagon I was driving had a two-way radio mounted under the dashboard. Our government cars in Cincinnati didn't have dashboard radios, so I had never used one.

"OK," I asked, "how do I do that?"

David then began giving me instructions. He showed me how to turn it on, select the correct frequency, depress the red button, and speak into the microphone. Then he told me what to say. I was supposed to say, "Crown, this is Grand 1, departing Sunflower in route to Sunshine." Crown was the communication center located in the White House in Washington, DC, Grand 1 was David's code name, Sunflower was the code name for Major John's residence, and Sunshine was the code name for President Eisenhower's farmhouse. (The code name for the Gettysburg Detail itself was the Mahjong Detail.)

Once we arrived at our destination, which only took five minutes, I had to let everyone know that we'd arrived safely by again calling in: "Crown, this is Grand 1, arriving Sunshine." I had just completed my first on-the-job training lesson on protection. It was taught to me by the eleven-year-old child (three days before his twelfth birthday) whom I was supposed to be protecting.

The president's farm had its own 24-7 security detail provided by the White House Police out of Washington, so I wasn't too worried. Someone here had to know what they were doing. David walked over to a security office, where he grabbed a basketball and told the security officer that we would be around in back of the house.

As the two of us headed that way, David dribbled the ball and asked, "Do you like basketball?" I told him that I did, and that in fact it was my favorite sport after golf. "Do you want to shoot some baskets?" he asked, and I replied, "Sure, why not?"

There was a cement pad with a basketball hoop located outside the kitchen window behind the farmhouse. David started dribbling and taking some shots. He then passed me the ball, and the two of us started taking turns shooting and passing the ball back and forth. We did this for a few minutes when I asked David if he knew how to play horse. It's a game where each player takes a shot until one player makes a basket, and then the other player has to match the same shot. If that player makes the same shot, there is no penalty; however, if he misses, he gets his first letter, *H*. The game continues until a player misses enough times to spell out the word H-O-R-S-E and is eliminated. This goes on and on until the last remaining person is finally declared the winner. Since there were only two of us playing, a game went by rather quickly.

Up to this point, I had been wearing my sport coat, which was cramping my style, so I decided to take it off and set it aside along with my holster and .38 Special. *Much better*, I thought as we resumed playing. The two of us continued to take crazy shots, trying to make the other one miss, and I stopped paying attention to my surroundings. After all, we were alone and secure in the center of this big farm. Who, other than the White House Detail, could possibly know we were there?

My heart jumped when a voice coming from behind me said "Hello, David" and David replied "Hi, Granddad."

I turned around and standing right there, no more than ten feet away, was President Dwight D. Eisenhower, the most powerful man in the world. For a moment, I was dumbfounded. I had actually allowed someone to get within ten feet of us without even knowing they were there, and it was the president of the United States no less. I wondered if I had blown my temporary assignment in my first hour on protection.

After regaining my composure, I slipped over to the side of the basketball court, where I picked up my weapon, covered it with my sport coat, and walked back to the security office, where I waited, along with other agents from the White House Detail, for President Eisenhower and David to finish their visit. Nothing was ever said, but I knew I had blundered big time. Another on-the-job training lesson: pay attention to your surroundings at all times, no matter where you are and how secure you feel. Still, I wondered why I hadn't been told about the president's visit in the first place. It didn't matter; I should have been alert anyway.

David had school the next day, so his visit with Granddad didn't last long. We departed Sunshine and returned to Sunflower, where I completed my four-to-midnight shift sitting in a station wagon parked in front of the Eisenhower residence. There were two station wagons, one that we drove and one that stayed parked and served as our "office."

Usually, five agents were on duty at the same time, one for each grandchild and one for the residence, but that first evening, since everyone was in, there were only two of us. When my shift ended at midnight and I returned to my motel room, I didn't feel the least bit tired, but as soon as my head hit the pillow, with the events of the day swirling through my head, I was out like a light. It had been an eventful fifteen hours, starting that morning at the Treasury Building in Washington, DC. I had to be back on duty at 8:00 AM, but I didn't mind. I was doing something new and exciting, and I was hooked. I knew that protection was where I wanted to be.

For the rest of my first week in Gettysburg, I was on day shift. The day shift usually involved following the school bus, with the grandchildren on board, to Keefauver Elementary School, a private school in Gettysburg. While class was in session, I sat in a chair outside the classroom door and monitored the hallway. It reminded me of when I was in elementary school and sat in the hallway outside of my classroom, only then it wasn't for monitoring. During recess, I stood outside on the playground or in the gym talking with the teachers.

My second week I was on midnights, and midnights were dull. Three of us took turns rotating between our office, which was a Ford station wagon parked in front of the house, and a four-foot-by-four-foot security booth located at a corner of the backyard behind the house. I was on the midnight shift when I learned that we would be spending Easter weekend in Augusta, Georgia, with President Eisenhower. The President had a seven-room, three-story, full-basement house that was built for him near the tenth tee of the world-famous Augusta National Golf Course, site of the annual Masters golf tournament. The Secret Service code name for the house was Cabin, and they used the basement as a headquarters whenever the president was in residence.

Being an avid golfer, I was excited. What a great temporary assignment this was turning out to be. On the morning of April 14, 1960, after working the midnight shift, three other agents and I drove from Gettysburg to the White House in DC with the four grandchildren in two of our official vehicles. The grandchildren spent the night in the White House, where I was again on midnight duty. In the morning, I was transported to Bolling AFB and boarded an air force plane for the two-and-three-quarter-hour flight from DC to Augusta, Georgia. I was with a group of other off-duty agents, and we all checked into the Richmond Hotel, where reservations had already been confirmed.

The president and his grandchildren flew separately on the *Columbine II*, a Lockheed VC-121A LO Constellation. That particular airplane was the first presidential aircraft to use the Air Force One call sign as a security precaution, because of an earlier near-incident with an Eastern Air Lines commercial flight that had the same call sign as a flight the president was on. First Lady Mamie Eisenhower had named the airplane *Columbine* after the Colorado state flower, because of some sentimental ties that she had with Colorado.

I was still assigned to midnight duty, but after catching a couple of hours of sleep and a meal at the hotel, I hitched an early ride to beautiful Augusta National with the 4:00 PM–midnight shift. They were short on agents, so I was assigned to help fill in. I didn't mind. I was just eager to get a glimpse of Augusta National in the daylight. At midnight, I switched back to the children's detail, and I spent the night inside the entrance to the grandchildren's cottage, which was located a short distance from Cabin, the president's residence.

When I came off my midnight shift at 8:00 AM on Saturday morning, I was told that President Eisenhower was going to play golf. The President's Detail was short on agents, and I was told that I had just "volunteered" to fill in. I was unfamiliar with how the President's Detail worked but was told not to worry. "Just go over to the front of the clubhouse, look for the presidential limo, and wait there. Someone will tell you what to do."

I located the limo parked in front of the pro shop. SAIC Jerry Behn introduced himself, as did SA Bill Greer, SA Sam Kinney, and ATSAIC John Campion. I remembered seeing Behn and Campion at the farm in Gettysburg on my first day on temporary assignment. I hoped they didn't remember me. When SAIC Behn opened the trunk of the limo, I peered in and saw an assortment of weapons. A Thompson submachine gun was the first to catch my eye. I had never seen a tommy gun in person before, other than in gangster movies of the 1930s and '40s.

SAIC Behn then reached into the trunk and pulled out a golf bag. He looked around our assembly of agents and handed it to me. The golf bag was vintage, probably late 1930s or early 1940s. It held three golf clubs: a hickory-shafted mashie (5/7 iron), a hickory-shafted niblick (9 iron/wedge), and an enamel-shafted spoon (3 wood). That was all that was visible. It was all very out of date for 1960, and to me it really looked stupid. Hidden inside the bag was a .30 caliber M1 carbine, the official weapon of the

Special Agent Paul Landis with a Thompson submachine gun, Middleburg, Virginia. *Author's collection*

US Marine Corps during World War II. I didn't even know how to get the M1 carbine out of the bag, let alone shoot it.

I was then told to go to the first tee and wait there for further instructions. I hefted the bag, placing the strap over my right shoulder, and headed off to the first tee and the unknown.

When Ike's foursome was spotted approaching the first tee, I was told to head down along the rough on the right side of the fairway and to keep an eye out for intruders. I was to stay about 250 yards ahead of the players and follow this procedure as play progressed around the golf course. The first hole was around 365 yards long, and as I headed down toward the green I kept looking back over my shoulder to see how everyone was doing and noticed that things were not going well. I stopped about fifty feet behind the green and waited, not wanting to get too far ahead of the group.

All four golfers were playing badly. Even the president was hacking. After the foursome finally reached the green and holed out, they replaced the flag and were having a big discussion on the green. My curiosity was aroused, so I eased closer to the green, hoping to learn what was going on.

Since all four golfers, including President Eisenhower, had started out playing so poorly, they had agreed to put the first hole behind them and start over. What they couldn't agree on was how to do it. Should they go back to the first tee to start over, or should they continue on to the second tee and restart from there? There was a lot of head shaking, pointing back and forth between the first and second tee, and so on.

I got so caught up in the drama that I became negligent in my assignment. I was mentally transposing this scene back to the White House, where I envisioned it taking place in the situation room. In my vision, the president was there surrounded by his White House staff and advisers. The secretary of state, the director of the National Security Council, the secretary of defense, the chairman of the Joint Chiefs of Staff, everyone of importance that you could imagine were all there. They were all huddled over a table with a model of Augusta National Golf Course before them, and no one could agree on what to do.

I thought the scene that I had created in my mind was quite humorous, and I was chuckling to myself when I heard, "Landis," and suddenly snapped out of my reverie. I looked over to my right and saw ATSAIC John Campion stomping my way, his face beet red. "Landis," he repeated, "if the attack comes, it's going to come from behind you, *not* from the green." ATSAIC Campion had embarrassed me in front of everyone, even the president, and I felt about knee-high to a grasshopper.

About that time, the president and his "staff" decided to continue on from where they were, so I scampered ahead down the second fairway eager to get ahead of the group *and* ahead of ATSAIC Campion. I later learned that ATSAIC Campion's code name was Dragon. I knew why.

I finished the round without further incident and even managed to find a golf ball in the process. Nothing was ever said, but I knew that I had repeated the same mistake that I had made on my first day at the president's farm. I had to remember to always be alert and keep an eye on the surroundings, no matter what.

When the president finished his round of golf, I got a ride back to the hotel to catch up on some needed sleep. I had to be back again for my midnight shift with the grandchildren. By the way, no one went back to replay the first hole either.

It was Easter Sunday morning when I got off the midnight shift. I was told to go back to the hotel and change into a suit and tie, return, and be prepared to attend Easter services with the president's grandchildren. I was on short shift change that Sunday, meaning that I also had to work again from 4:00 PM to midnight. So, after church it was back to the hotel again for a short nap and then back to Augusta National.

The next morning, Monday, I returned to Washington on the *Columbine* along with the president and the grandchildren and continued on to Gettysburg by car. For the remainder of the month, the daily routine was the same as before Easter.

On April 30, 1960, my temporary assignment complete, SA Iacovoni rejoined me for the return trip to Cincinnati.

When I walked into the Cincinnati Field Office on Monday, May 2, 1960, the first thing SAIC McCann did was greet me with a smile on his face and hand me a memo dated April 22, 1960. It was from Chief U. E. Baughman, and it read:

SA Paul E. Landis, Jr.—Transfer to the Gettysburg Detail
Please advise SA Landis that he will be transferred
to the Gettysburg Detail on June 1, 1960
for permanent assignment, and should arrange
to report to ATSAIC Barton on that date.

Despite my previous blunders, I was headed back, and I was elated.

———————

When I returned to Gettysburg, it felt like I had never been gone. I was immediately accepted as a full-time member of the team. Special Agents David Grant and Horace "Harry" Gibbs invited me to share their apartment, a two-story walk-up on Carlisle Street, right by the railroad tracks and across from the train station. Every time a train went through, the whole apartment rattled, but I didn't care.

What I learned that summer was the camaraderie that existed among all the agents, not only those of us in Gettysburg but all agents on all details. There was a common bond. All our various dispositions, personalities, and interests made no difference. Everyone got along. Everyone worked together and played together. There was no moaning or complaining. There was always a group activity of some kind to attend—a family picnic, bachelors included, or a weekend softball game. Some of us were hunters and golfers. We had a bowling team that participated in a local league. I even met a local crop duster who gave me flying lessons for five dollars an hour.

The daily routine had changed now that the grandchildren were on summer break from school. Horseback riding and swimming lessons had replaced sitting outside of classrooms. Baseball games, visiting friends, and going to the Gettysburg Country Club replaced hanging around a playground during recess.

In mid-July four of us, SA Harry Gibbs, SA David Grant, SA Earl Moore, and myself, all bachelors, took a trip to Dewey Beach, Delaware, so that David Eisenhower could visit Kenny Wherry, a buddy from St. Stephen's Episcopal School in Alexandria, Virginia. We spent five days sunning and playing catch on the beach and swimming in the Atlantic Ocean. We went crabbing and ate steamed crabs in the evening, all of us sitting together around the kitchen table. We were treated like family, so it was more like a mini vacation than a protective assignment. What made it easier, too, was the fact that no one else knew we were there, and no one recognized David.

On August 2, after spending a night in the White House, all four grandchildren left DC with President Eisenhower for four days in Newport, Rhode Island. The president vacationed at the "Summer White House" located on Naval Station Newport. All of the detail agents had accommodations in the officers' quarters. Ironically, this is where I would have been stationed for training if I had entered Officer Candidate School two years earlier. It is also where David Eisenhower would attend Officer Candidate School in the future.

All agents ate their meals in the officers' mess, which is where I met Special Agent Tom Wells. When I first saw Tom, I thought that I had finally found an agent younger than me, but no such luck. He only looked younger, so as far as I knew, I was still the youngest kid on the block.

Five days after returning to Gettysburg, we were back in DC for two weeks. The president suffered one of his many heart attacks and was hospitalized at Walter Reed Hospital. The grandchildren and their mother, Barbara Jean Eisenhower, stayed in the White House. The agents from Gettysburg stayed at a nearby boarding-house called "Ma Buma's." We spent our time shuttling the grand-children back and forth between the White House, Walter Reed,

Special Agent Paul Landis, age twenty-five, with President Eisenhower's grandchildren, Newport, Rhode Island, Labor Day weekend 1960. Left to right: Barbara Anne Eisenhower, Special Agent Larry Hess, Susan Eisenhower, David Eisenhower, and Special Agent Paul Landis. *Author's collection, photographer unknown*

and friends in the area. In August, I even got to take David to a night baseball game at Griffith Stadium. However, when things were quiet, we spent most of our time sitting around in the Secret Service office just off the West Wing.

On one of those evenings when I was on the 4:00 PM–midnight shift, I was lounging on the couch in the Secret Service office talking with Assistant Special Agent in Charge (ASAIC) Floyd Boring about my golf bag experience in Augusta, Georgia. I noted that both the golf bags and the clubs in them really needed to be updated. I mentioned the M1 carbine too. I was a member of the National Rifle Association and received their monthly magazine, *American Rifleman*. I had read about a new lightweight assault rifle that Colt's Manufacturing and Armalite were developing for use in Vietnam. It was called the AR-15, and it fired a small .223 caliber high-velocity round. I thought it would be a perfect fit for the Secret Service, to replace both our M1 carbines and our tommy guns. This was all new information to ASAIC Boring, so on the following evening I brought all the information in for him to read and to possibly pass along to the higher-ups. After returning to Gettysburg with the Kiddie Detail, I never gave it another thought.

Months later I learned that the AR-15 had become an official weapon of the Secret Service. I know that no matter what anyone else thinks, says, or did, on that August evening in 1960, I planted the seed for the AR-15 to become the Secret Service's weapon of choice. I don't care who took credit for it; that's one lasting contribution that I am proud of.

Summer ended with a long Labor Day weekend at Patuxent Point, Maryland, sailing on the presidential yachts *Barbara Anne* and *Susie E*, which President Kennedy renamed the *Honey Fitz* and the *Patrick J* after he was elected president.

From September 19 through October 28, 1960, I attended Treasury Law Enforcement Officer Training School, my first formal training of any kind. At that time, the Treasury Department oversaw seven law enforcement agencies: the US Customs Service, the US Coast Guard, the US Secret Service, the Bureau of Narcotics, the IRS–Intelligence Division, the IRS–Alcohol and Tobacco Tax Division, and the IRS–Inspection Division. Agents from each of the seven attended from all over the country.

There were five of us representing the Secret Service: SA Ernie Olson, Kansas City, Missouri; SA Bob Snow, Buffalo, New York; SA Bob Till, Columbus, Ohio; SA Ken Wiesman, Houston, Texas; and me, Gettysburg, Pennsylvania. We learned the various functions of all seven law enforcement divisions as well as the many investigative techniques that we would probably use at some point in our careers in the Treasury Department. A *great* emphasis was placed on report writing. We also practiced self-defense and spent hours in the indoor pistol range perfecting our accuracy with our handguns. It was a fantastic learning experience, and I was happy to finally do something other than OJT. Another interesting feature of our training sessions was the ten-minute smoke break after every hour of instruction. Just about everybody smoked then, and it makes me want to cough now just thinking about it.

After Treasury School, all special agents returned to their various departments to await additional specialty training that would apply more directly to their own work. I returned to the midnight–8:00 AM shift in Gettysburg.

On November 8, 1960, John F. Kennedy was elected president of the United States. All of the agents in Gettysburg wondered where we would end up, especially me.

It didn't take me long to find out. On November 17, 1960, I was notified that effective January 23, I would be assigned to the White House Detail in Washington, DC. In the meantime, I also learned that I would be attending Secret Service Training School from January 9 through February 10, 1961.

On Saturday, January 7, I finished my midnight shift, and before I left Sunflower for the last time, I took the opportunity to say good-bye to the Eisenhower grandchildren.

5

SECRET SERVICE SCHOOL
AND WHITE HOUSE DETAIL

SECRET SERVICE TRAINING SCHOOL took place at the W. & J. Sloane building, 711 Twelfth Street NW, in Washington, DC. On the first day, nineteen of us assembled on the fourth floor and were told that during the second week of school we would be given a comprehensive examination on the Secret Service Manual, followed by subsequent examinations on the Legal Opinions and Decisions Manual and the Production of Currency & Other Obligations of the United States Manual. Yikes! We were also told that we would be pulled out of school for two days for special assignments during the inauguration of President Kennedy (*yeah!*); however, the two days of class would be made up on two separate Saturdays (*boo!*).

Secret Service School was great. We visited the Crane Paper Company in Dalton, Massachusetts, where the special fiber paper for our US currency is made. We went to the Philadelphia Mint to learn how coinage is made, and also to the Bureau of Engraving, where our paper currency is printed, and learned how to identify counterfeit money. We spent many hours on the firing range increasing our weapons proficiency. The daily routine still included on-the-job-training, but I felt more confident knowing that my formal training would be behind me.

As we had previously been informed, on the eve of the inauguration (January 19) there was no school. Instead, our class met at the Treasury Building for a morning briefing on inaugural procedures, followed by a group photo taken on the front steps of the building. After lunch, we all reported back to the Washington Field Office (WFO) for possible assignments. I was sent to the Sheraton Park Hotel for an afternoon governor's reception and then to Constitution Hall to cover an evening dinner. On Friday, Inauguration Day, I spent the morning assigned to post #24, which covered the area of Pennsylvania Avenue between Thirteenth and Fourteenth Streets. In the afternoon, I was posted in front of the reviewing stand located on Pennsylvania Avenue in front of the White House. That evening I was sent to the DC Armory and was not released from duty until 2:00 AM the following morning.

Secret Service School ended on Friday, February 10. From this point on, all my training would be OJT, except for maintaining my handgun proficiency. That was up to me personally. Whenever I was in DC and had the opportunity, I went to the pistol range in the basement of the Treasury Building. Several other agents did the same, and sometimes there were not enough earmuffs to go around, so we would put bullets in our ears for protection. It looked pretty stupid, and we laughed about it, but it worked. Never underestimate the resourcefulness of a Secret Service agent.

I reported to the White House at 6:30 AM on Sunday, February 12, for transportation to Middleburg, Virginia, where President Kennedy was spending his first weekend in office with the First Lady. I worked with the day shift and continued with my scheduled 4:00 PM–midnight shift at Glen Ora, a farm

Mrs. Kennedy had rented. It was a long first day, but I didn't mind. I was on protection and assigned to the White House Detail.

My first face-to-face with President Kennedy didn't occur until more than a week later, because I had been on the midnight and the 4:00 PM–midnight shifts. Starting Monday, February 20, I was finally on the day shift. My post was at the end of a walkway that leads from the West Wing and Oval Office to the main living quarters of the White House. The Rose Garden sits on one side of the walkway, and the enclosed White House swimming pool, now gone, was located along the other side. The president was walking toward me, engrossed in conversation with someone and not really paying attention to anything else. I opened the door for them and said, "Good morning, Mr. President." He glanced at me, smiled, nodded his head, and continued walking and talking. I thought nothing more about it.

On the following day I was at the same post when the president again came through, only this time he was headed toward the West Wing and he was alone. As he passed by, I again said, "Good morning, Mr. President."

This time he replied, "Good morning, Mr. Landis." You could have knocked me over with a feather. This man, the president of the United States, had gone to the trouble to learn who I was. And it wasn't just me. He did that with all the agents. He made the effort to learn all of our names. That's the kind of person he was, and it left a great impression on me.

Easter fell on April 2 that year, and I was in Palm Beach, Florida, with the First Family. They were spending the weekend with Joseph P. and Rose Kennedy, the president's parents. Another Easter holiday and I again found myself on a golf course, just like the year before with President Eisenhower. This time it was with President Kennedy and the famous male baritone Bing Crosby.

We were at the Palm Beach Country Club, and I had the same assignment as the year earlier: keeping ahead of the golfers. But things were looking up. I was now carrying a newer golf bag with three newer clubs and a shotgun instead of an M1 carbine. I was also minding my p's and q's, but I did manage to sneak a peek once in a while to watch Bing. I heard that he was an excellent golfer, and from what I saw, it was true. He had a beautiful golf swing, consistently hitting the ball straight down the middle of the fairway. He was a real pleasure to watch, and I only wished I could play as well.

Later that month, on April 27, we flew to New York City for an overnight visit. We stayed at the Carlyle Hotel, where the president had a suite on the thirty-fourth floor. The Carlyle is an elegant luxury hotel located at East Seventy-Sixth Street and Madison Avenue on the Upper East Side of Manhattan. The hotel was extremely expensive, but because all agents were on a limited per diem rate of twelve dollars per day, the Secret Service and management negotiated an unbelievable rate of five dollars per night.

I was happy to be living around DC and especially pleased with my new assignment. Energy seemed to pulse through every artery and from every pore of the nation's capital, and I was a part of it. I was patriotic to the core and proud of my country, and now I was serving at its very heart, the White House.

Days were exciting—buzzing around Washington, accompanying the president to various venues like the State Department or visiting hotels for meetings and speeches. However, midnight shifts at the White House were another thing altogether. *Boooor- ing.* We were not allowed to read on post, so I used to while away the time counting the holes in the acoustic ceiling tiles outside the Oval Office, or the number of floor tiles in the hallway between the Oval Office and the press secretary's office. I was usually relieved by another agent before I could finish, so the next time around I would start all over again. I even tried to dream up pranks to trick the agent who would be relieving me, but most of those were too risky to do, and I probably would have lost my job on the spot.

Midnights at the Glen Ora farm in Middleburg, Virginia, were even worse. Sitting alone in a small security booth in the middle of the woods, in the dark, in the dead of night, could get creepy. Hearing the different sounds of the night could play tricks on the imagination, so I had to be careful not to overreact.

Whenever the First Family traveled to Glen Ora, they always brought along Charlie, their pet Welsh terrier. Charlie loved to play fetch, so much so that he could be a real pain. One weekend when I was on duty at Glen Ora, Charlie got me really good. I was on the midnight shift in the security booth. It was quiet outside, and there was no moon. Suddenly there was a loud *kerplunk* inside the booth. It startled the living bejesus out of me, and I jumped, my heart racing.

It was Charlie. He was outside for the night and had rummaged up a croquet ball. He was looking for someone to play fetch with. I happened to be the victim of choice. I did not see or hear him sneak up on me until the wooden ball suddenly landed on the wooden floor of the security booth. I was so mad, I picked up the ball and threw it away as hard as I could.

I stepped back inside the booth and was still stewing when, a few minutes later, *kerplunk*. He was back. He had found the ball and wanted me to throw it again. Considering the situation, I couldn't help but laugh to myself. "You got me, Charlie. You got me good." So, giving in, the two of us ended up playing fetch until my relief came.

The president and First Lady signed a two-year lease agreement for Glen Ora. It was now an official presidential residence and required security around the clock. That meant another detail. An SAIC was put in charge, and special agents from the White House Detail and from field offices around the country were brought in on temporary ninety-day assignments to provide that coverage. On April 29, 1961, my number came up, and I was transferred to the Glen Ora Detail. I was still considered a part of the White House Detail, but I would not be traveling with "the Boss," as the president was known. At least I didn't have to move, because Glen Ora was an easy forty-seven-mile daily commute from my apartment in Arlington.

The Secret Service commandeered a stable located next to a tack room on the farm and converted it into office space. The White House Army Signal Agency also set up a communications center that could reach out to anywhere in the world. Security booths were constructed and placed at various observation points around the property.

Because Glen Ora was so secluded, when the First Family was not in residence, the atmosphere was a little more relaxed. It had an outdoor swimming pool and cabana located beside a flat grassy area that was used as a helipad whenever the president traveled to and from the White House. With the assistance of the Army Signal Agency personnel, we made sure that the pool area was always kept secure, especially on warm, sunny days, whenever a member of the First Family was not in residence.

During the daylight and evening shifts, another special agent and I would patrol the area, making rounds in a jeep. We practiced our marksmanship shooting at groundhogs, rationalizing that we were doing the proprietors a favor by eliminating the pesky critters that were making dangerous holes that horses could trip in and break a leg. One day the local game warden, Gene, showed up to see what all the racket was, making sure nothing illegal was going on.

Special Agent Paul Landis reporting for work, Middleburg, Virginia, summer 1961. *Author's collection*

Gene and I became good friends, and he introduced me to several of the area property owners, who allowed me to hunt and fish on their farms. I always kept a fishing rod and small tackle box handy, just in case an opportunity to use them presented itself. Sometimes at night when I wasn't on duty, I would patrol with Gene, searching for poachers who would be out spotlighting for deer. He appreciated the company, and I enjoyed the excitement.

I took advantage of the contacts I had made through Gene, too, and fished the nearby farm ponds whenever possible. Farm ponds were seldom fished and at times could be very productive.

Fishing was always important to me. Later when I was assigned to the Kiddie Detail, I returned to Glen Ora with the children and Mrs. Kennedy for a weekend. The weather was gorgeous on Saturday, May 5, 1962. I'd spent the day out with Caroline, and we were finishing up for the day. I decided that I was going to take advantage of the beautiful, quiet spring evening and try fishing a pond that I knew about located on Colonel McCoy's nearby farm. I retrieved a bucket and my fishing tackle from the stable area and was getting ready to load it into the trunk of a car when Mrs. Kennedy and Caroline happened to come out of the house and spotted me.

Mrs. Kennedy approached and asked me what I was doing. While I was explaining, Caroline started jumping up and down, asking, "Can I come along? Can I go, can I go?"

Then Mrs. Kennedy asked me, "Mr. Landis, do you mind if we tag along too?" Well, talk about being put on the spot.

What am I supposed to say? I thought. *"Sorry, Mrs. Kennedy, but I want to spend a quiet evening alone"?* How on earth could I ever do that, and why would I even want to say no to the First Lady? Besides, I was flattered and excited at the thought that she was interested enough to want to come along. The three of us piled into the car, and it was *Colonel McCoy, here we come.*

The McCoy farm was located off a gravel road, not too far from Glen Ora. When we arrived, I parked next to a faded red barn and grabbed my fishing rod and bucket from the trunk. The pond was only a short hike away in the middle of an overgrown pasture. I had preselected a red-and-white Jitterbug as my casting lure, so I was good to go. The three of us headed across the field, with me leading the way. When we reached the pond, I set my bucket down and immediately started working my way around the edge, casting into the pond slightly ahead of me.

Caroline was more interested in the frogs, turtles, tadpoles, and butterflies, so Mrs. Kennedy stayed and poked around with her while I fished. I was opposite them on the other side of the pond when I got a strike. I had cast the Jitterbug and was looking up to check on their whereabouts when a five-plus-pound largemouth bass struck my bait. I set the hook, and when the fish leaped out of the water I noticed that the swivel snap attached to the bait had become unhooked. One good leap and I would lose the fish, Jitterbug and all. However, I was more concerned about being embarrassed in front of the First Lady.

I managed to land the fish, and Mrs. Kennedy and Caroline clapped their hands and cheered. I was elated. I had the fish mounted in remembrance of that day, and it still hangs on my office wall. That's just another example of what it was like to be around the Kennedys. They took a personal interest in everyone. They cared.

Author's collection

6

MY DEBUT

M Y INITIAL NINETY-DAY ASSIGNMENT at Middleburg ended on
July 23, 1961, and I was happy to be back at the White
House. I was there a whole week before I learned that I was going
to Hyannis Port, Massachusetts. My new assignment was at a six-
acre, three-house complex of prime waterfront and beach property
on Cape Cod overlooking Nantucket Sound. The Kennedy family's
patriarch and matriarch, Joe and Rose Kennedy, owned a large
summer home there. The president and his brother Robert each
owned their own separate houses on the property. There was an
outdoor swimming pool by Robert's house and a helipad area in
front of Joe's main house. A private pier jutted out into the sound.
The entire complex was known as the Kennedy Compound.

Security arrangements at the Compound were pretty much
the same as at Glen Ora. There was a security office behind the
president's garage, a communications center, and security booths
located at various spots around the perimeter of the property. The
Secret Service detail was larger, because of the nature of the property, but the routine was the same—swing shifts and rotations.

Robert Kennedy and his family had a pet Newfoundland dog
named Brumus. He was a big lug of a dog with long black fur and
the disposition of a pussycat. Brumus spent the nights outside,

and his favorite place to sleep was across a pathway the agents used when changing observation posts. His black coat blended into the night, and it only took me two times tripping over him on the midnight shift before I wised up. There must be a lesson here about me, dogs, and midnights.

All of the president's siblings had homes nearby, but the focal point was the Compound. During the days and evenings, most of the president's nieces and nephews were there swimming and playing together. Caroline was approaching the age of four, and John Jr. was now nine months old, walking and becoming more mobile. This necessitated an expanded Kiddie Detail. On August 22, 1961, after only three weeks in Hyannis Port, I was informed that I was the necessity.

Special Agent Paul Landis at the Kennedy Compound dock, Hyannis Port, Massachusetts, August 1961. *Author's collection*

Until now, the Kennedy Kiddie Detail had consisted of two special agents, SA Lynn Meredith and SA Bob Foster, my friend from Worthington who had inspired me to join the Secret Service. My new position required a code name, one that I could use for security and identification purposes. My code name was selected for me. I had no input in the process.

Not all agents required code names, but for those agents who did, during the Kennedy years, the codes began with the letter *D* and in some way or another tended to match an agent's personality—like ATSAIC John Campion's code name, Dragon. Clint Hill was Dazzle, based on his sparkling eyes and film-star looks. Lynn Meredith was Drummer, because of his musical talent. Bob Foster's penchant for clothes earned him the code name Dresser. My code name became Debut, both because of my youth and because this assignment was considered my coming-out party. I was still the youngest agent on the White House Detail. I knew that I didn't look anywhere near my age of twenty-six, so it was OK with me. Incidentally, the First Family's code names all began with the letter "L." The president was Lancer, Mrs. Kennedy was Lace, Caroline was Lyric, and John Jr. was Lark.

I spent the next fourteen months on the Kiddie Detail, also known as the Diaper Detail. Many agents may have thought of it as a lesser assignment, more like a glorified babysitting job, but for me, protecting the president and Mrs. Kennedy's children was both important and (mostly) fun. I focused on the positives, like no more swing shifts and no more midnights. These kids weren't going anywhere after dark, and when they were in residence at the White House, they would be the responsibility of the regular White House Detail.

Washington was considered my home assignment. Whenever I was away from DC, I received my twelve-dollar per diem allowance to cover extra expenses. This may not seem like much by today's

Paul Landis and John Jr., Middleburg,
Virginia, 1961. *Author's collection*

standards, but at that time, it was a nice bonus. I was a bachelor
without much in the way of expenses, and because the children
spent a lot of time away from DC, the per diems soon added up.
For me, Kiddie Detail was like being on paid vacation with a bonus.

The Kiddie Detail tended to float with the seasons. At the end
of a summer in Hyannis Port, we would move on to Newport,
Rhode Island, to visit Mrs. Kennedy's mother and stepfather, Janet
and Hugh Auchincloss, at Hammersmith Farm, the estate where
Mrs. Kennedy had grown up. After a month or so in Newport,
it was off to Palm Beach for most of the winter. Then, in spring,
it would be back to the White House, spending weekends in
Middleburg, Virginia. Various trips back and forth to DC were
interspersed from each location.

My first trip to Palm Beach on the Kiddie Detail was in December 1961. I was there on Tuesday, December 19, when Joseph P. Kennedy, the president's father, had a stroke. The president flew down from Washington to check on his father, flew back to DC, and then returned to Palm Beach over the weekend for the Christmas holiday. While in Florida, the president made daily visits to St. Mary's Hospital in West Palm Beach to visit his father, driving himself in a favorite white Lincoln convertible. One day I was outside with Caroline when the president stopped to ask her if she wanted to go see Grandpa and help cheer him up. She ran and jumped in with her father. I ran to the follow-up car.

When we arrived at the hospital, everyone swarmed into the lobby with the president and Caroline, but the entourage stopped there. I was selected to be the lone agent to go up with the president and Caroline while they visited with Grandpa. We rode up in the elevator together, and when we reached Joseph Kennedy's

Mrs. Kennedy greets the president on his arrival at West Palm Beach Airport, December 1961. *Author's collection*

floor, I followed them to his room, and then I returned to the nurse's station and waited.

When their visit was over, I escorted them into the elevator and down to the first floor, where everyone else was waiting. As the elevator doors opened, Caroline spotted a gumball machine across the hallway, directly in front of the elevator. "Daddy, Daddy," she exclaimed, in an excited voice, while tugging on his hand. "Can I have a gumball? Please, Daddy, please."

The president reached into his pocket—nothing. He then turned to me and said, "Mr. Landis, do you have a penny I can borrow?" I reached into my pocket and came up with some small change and handed the president a penny. He walked over to the gumball machine with Caroline. She inserted the penny, turned the dial, and retrieved a blue gumball. I could hardly believe that this kid from Worthington, Ohio, had to lend a penny to the president of the United States, the most powerful man in the world. I had just saved the day and probably helped avoid a major world crisis. Incidentally, I never got my penny back.

Caroline had a pony she called Macaroni. Macaroni was a ten-year-old roan, part-Shetland gelding. The Kennedys kept Macaroni stabled at Glen Ora farm. He was looked after there by David Lloyd, the caretaker. Occasionally, Lloyd would load Macaroni into a horse trailer and haul him to the White House so that Caroline could ride there. A small shelter was provided for Macaroni along the east side of the White House, but more frequently, Macaroni was allowed to roam and graze freely on the lush grass of the South Lawn.

Whenever Caroline wanted to ride Macaroni, it was the duty of the Kiddie Detail to look after her safety, which mostly consisted of guiding the two of them around on a lead rope. Caroline usually wanted to go faster, and that meant running. On one beautiful spring day, I happened to be the lead runner. An Associated Press photographer had been lurking outside the South Lawn fence, and he took a telephoto picture of us. The next day, March 21, 1962, the *Washington Evening Star* featured a front-page photograph of the three of us—Caroline, Macaroni, and me—caught in mid stride, passing in front of an entrance near the South Portico. The photograph was picked up by newspapers across the country.

A few days later, I received a framed copy of that photo. It included a note that read, "The four-minute mile—for Mr. Landis—with admiration! Jacqueline Kennedy." It had an additional note inscribed in a four-year-old's handwriting, "Love from Caroline."

Author's collection

Another time, after we had just finished our jog around the south grounds, Caroline said to me, "I want to go see Daddy."

Rather than tell her "No, that's not a good idea" and that Daddy was probably busy in his office, I figured, *Why not?* So, rope in hand, I led Macaroni, with Caroline astride, past the Rose Garden and over to the Oval Office. It was another beautiful spring day, and the outside door to the Oval Office was open but the screen door was closed, allowing only fresh air to enter. I peeked around the corner and saw that the president was alone, sitting behind his desk, head down, busily writing away. He appeared to be deep in thought and had apparently not heard our approach. I hesitated for a moment, thinking to myself, *Hmm, I'll give it a shot.* Reaching out, I opened the screen door, and in we marched. I had the rope in my hand at one end and Caroline atop Macaroni at the other end. The president looked up, and if you could have seen the expression on his face—it was priceless. His jaw literally dropped open in utter disbelief.

I, of course, was wearing a big smile. President Kennedy pushed his chair away from his desk and started coming around to greet us. By now the shock of our grand entry had vanished and he was smiling from ear-to-ear. He came over to us, gave Caroline a hug, and, still smiling, turned to me and said, "Mr. Landis, I really don't think this is a good idea."

By then I was starting to have second thoughts too. What if Macaroni started peeing on the huge presidential-seal rug in the Oval Office or, worse yet, making piles of doo-doo? I knew that if Macaroni started to do that, I'd be in deep doo-doo too. We managed to exit the Oval Office without incident, and I wandered off with Macaroni in tow while the president stayed behind and talked with Caroline. I am willing to bet that no one else has ever taken a horse into the Oval Office.

Maud Shaw was the children's nanny. She had been the nanny for Caroline before President Kennedy's election, and she came to the White House with them when they moved in. She was friendly and easy to get along with, and we relied on her a lot for advance notice of any plans for the children. She liked taking the children away from the White House, and we spent many hours wandering in Montrose Park or Rose Park, both in Georgetown. The two parks were relatively safe areas, and we were usually unrecognized or left alone. We occasionally went to the National Zoological Park, but the situation there was entirely different. The zoo was more public, so it didn't take long before Caroline and John Jr. would be recognized and the word would spread. The crowd of onlookers would grow, and we would stay only as long as it remained tolerable. Eventually, we would have to leave.

John Jr., Caroline, and Maud Shaw, the children's governess, on the White House South Lawn, 1962. *Author's collection*

As the Kennedys migrated with the seasons, Maud Shaw developed her own daily agenda for the children, and we went along. During the summers in Hyannis Port, most activities focused around the Kennedy Compound—playing on the beach, swimming, or maybe Caroline's riding lessons at the Allen Farm in Osterville, Massachusetts. On days off, I even managed to take in a few free riding lessons for myself.

In the fall at Hammersmith Farm, we would go where Shaw wanted to take the children, places like the Breakers, Bailey's Beach, or the Swiss Village, a small reproduction of a village in Switzerland. If the president came up from DC for a weekend visit and was cruising on the presidential yacht the *Honey Fitz* with the children on board, we tagged along, following in our jet runabout boats and chasing away other watercraft that came too close.

The first winter in Palm Beach was spent at Joseph and Rose Kennedy's house at 1095 North Ocean Boulevard, but the second winter Mrs. Kennedy rented a home from friends—Colonel C. Michael Paul and his wife, Josephine. It was close by, also on North Ocean Boulevard, but more private. That didn't change our daily routine with the children. We would drive to the west side of Palm Beach Island and then walk along Lake Trail, a scenic pathway that ran along the intercoastal waterway, or go to the beach. Spring found us back in DC, doing the usual park visits, plus weekend trips to Glen Ora farm.

All of the above activities were interspersed with trips back and forth to Washington, DC, either by car, military helicopter, or the Kennedys' private airplane, the *Caroline*, a Convair CV-240 piloted by Captain Howard Baird. We ended our spring tour with a three-day visit to Camp David, Maryland, over the Fourth of July holiday. Afterward, it was on to Cape Cod for the summer.

7

RAVELLO, ITALY

For the summer of 1962, the Kennedys rented a house in Hyannis Port from Mort Downey, the well-known singer of the 1920s–1940s. The house was located on Squaw Island Road, close to the Kennedy Compound but still far enough away to provide a little more privacy.

I'd been allowed to drive my Corvette back to the cape for that summer, and I arrived for duty at the Downey residence the morning of July 10. I was eagerly looking forward to another year with Caroline and John Jr. Both children were polite and well mannered and took directions with little fuss, which made protection easier and a lot lower pressure. Being with the children also gave the agents assigned to the Kiddie Detail a more intimate glimpse of life within the First Family. I was looking forward to a repeat performance of the previous year, and the best was yet to come.

The summer started just as I thought it would; however, this year riding lessons had become top priority, with almost daily visits to the Allen Farm in Osterville. Shortly after falling into our regular summer routine, I was informed that Mrs. Kennedy was planning a trip to Italy to meet her sister Princess Lee Radziwill. Caroline was also going along to see her three-year-old cousin Anthony, Princess Lee's son. Maud Shaw would be staying home with John Jr. while

Providencia "Provi" Paredes, Mrs. Kennedy's personal assistant, would also attend to Caroline during the trip. Someone from the Kiddie Detail had to go along, and I was one of the agents chosen. Awesome—I was going to Italy! I was one lucky SOB.

On Sunday, August 5, 1962, our entourage boarded Pan American Airways flight 110 at 9:30 PM, headed for Rome. It was a red-eye flight, and we arrived at the Eternal City the next morning at 10:30 AM local time. Mrs. Kennedy, Caroline, Provi, and SA Hill flew first class while I flew coach with SA Toby Chandler. After reaching Rome, everyone continued on to Salerno in a privately chartered plane— everyone except Toby and me, that is. The two of us met up with a driver in a rented car for the seven-and-a-half-hour drive to Ravello.

Our driver hailed from Salerno and was a *carabiniere*, a member of the Italian military police. He was assigned to us for our entire visit to act as an interpreter and help with protection. He gave us a quick drive-by tour of some of Rome's famous ruins before we headed south for Salerno.

We drove past the Colosseum. It wasn't as large as I had envisioned from pictures, but it was still pretty impressive. It had been completed almost nineteen hundred years ago, and it was hard for me to believe that part of the original structure was still standing. Tired from the flight, my mind wandered, and I thought of the past and envisioned gladiators in combat against lions or against each other, fighting for their lives. It seemed so surreal.

On an uplifting note, we also passed the Trevi Fountain, where legend has it dreams come true. I thought of the movie *Three Coins in the Fountain* and started unconsciously humming the theme song, which Frank Sinatra had made famous. There were other sites, too, but the drive through Rome occurred too quickly, and I was overwhelmed.

The next thing I knew, we were heading onto the autostrada. I had heard stories about the famous European highways and their lack of speed limits, and I was prepared for a routine hundred-mile-per-hour cruise. Unfortunately, that was asking a lot from our leased Fiat, so I just sat back and wished that I had my 1962 Corvette with me so I could put it through a real test. Our driver pointed out several World War II battlefronts we passed along the way. I was amazed at the number of buildings that still bore scars of war, where bullets had pockmarked their exterior walls.

The charter flight carrying Mrs. Kennedy et al. had arrived in Salerno hours ahead of us, and her sister, Princess Lee, and her family were already there to greet them. They all continued on to Ravello by car, and by the time we arrived in Salerno they were long gone.

We had about sixteen miles to go along the coast to reach Amalfi, and then another four miles of hairpin turns up a steep mountainside to Ravello (elevation 1,200 feet). These roads were no hundred-mile-per-hour highways. They were narrow and twisty and clung to the mountainside like grapes clinging to a vine. It appeared to be a harrowing drive to me, but our experienced driver had been over these roads many times before, and he took the curves with ease. I just concentrated on the awesome views of the Mediterranean Sea that seemed to appear around every turn.

When we finally reached Ravello, we made our entrance through a stone archway that was barely the width of a car. Our driver stopped, got out of the car, made a quick survey, got back in, and slowly squeezed our Fiat through. He did it in magnificent style, with only a few minor scrapes to the car, but minus a side-view mirror.

Mrs. Kennedy and the others were already settled into the rented villa, Villa l'Episcopio, a former bishop's residence once occupied by King Vittorio Emanuele III. So after our grand entrée, we went directly to the Hotel Palumbo, where all the agents were sharing rooms. Since the hotel was only a short walk from Villa l'Episcopio, I could check in first and then go see what was up at the villa.

Special Agent Paul Landis on the patio
balcony, Villa l'Episcopio, Ravello,
Italy, August 1962. *Author's collection*

The Hotel Palumbo was extravagant and expensive, and again
our advance agent, Special Agent Paul Rundle, had negotiated the
"Secret Service special"—five dollars per night. I was starting to
take this lifestyle for granted, too young and too naive to appreciate the fantastic opportunities being presented. All I cared about
was that my twelve-dollar per diem would still cover my expenses.

The *fattorino* (bellhop) who showed me to my room spoke
English, and before leaving he told me to place my shoes and
dirty laundry in the hallway outside the room before retiring for
the night. I did so. When I got up in the morning, I found that
my shoes had been polished and my laundry freshly washed and
neatly folded. There would be no laundromat worries on this trip.

I don't remember anything in particular about the room, other than that the bathroom had a bidet. I had heard of bidets, never seen one, and learned that they were quite common in Europe. I was learning all sorts of wondrous things on this trip, and I still had three weeks in Italy ahead of me. I wondered what other new discoveries awaited me.

I learned that the vacationing party had also rented a villa in Conca dei Marini, a small beachside town located about two miles from Amalfi, a ten-minute drive. However, for both privacy and security, it was easier to get there by boat, so we were provided with two powerful Riva speedboats, along with skippers, to whisk us across the bay for that purpose. They would stay and be at our disposal all day long.

For travel down the mountain to Amalfi, the car company Fiat provided us with two vehicles. Each could best be described as a cross between a beach buggy and an oversized golf cart. They were fun to drive and cleared the archways with room to spare. With transportation assured and a hint of what was to come, everyone settled in for the days ahead.

We only had seven special agents in Ravello, a much smaller contingent compared to when we were back in the USA, so local police and additional *carabinieri* from Salerno were recruited to assist us. All these arrangements—the villas, the hotel, the cars, the boats, the additional security, everything—were set up and handled by one person: our advance man, SA Paul Rundle. I couldn't imagine how he managed to coordinate everything, but by the time we left, the Italian police had tagged us Ravello agents "the Magnificent Seven."

Special Agent Clint Hill was the lone agent assigned to the First Lady, and there were three of us on hand from the Kiddie Detail, plus two agents from the White House Detail. We had a lot of overlapping duties, which I didn't mind. After all, we were a team, and we worked together and shared duties all the time.

As a result, I spent my first five days in Ravello assigned to Villa l'Episcopio, where Caroline and her cousin Anthony spent a lot of time playing inside. If everyone was out, I remained to secure the residence in their absence.

On August 12, my birthday, I finally got my first glimpse of the villa in Conca dei Marini. Caroline and I had ridden down the mountain in one of our fancy golf carts. We were accompanied by Luciano Grando, a *carabiniere* detective from Salerno, who was also assigned to Caroline for the duration of our visit. When we reached Amalfi, we boarded one of the speedboats and off we went.

As we approached Conca dei Marini, I searched the shores, noticing some buildings and a small beach, but we weren't headed that way. We were going past that area and heading toward a sheer rock cliff. High above the water I noticed an opening from which a narrow wrought-iron stairway and stone steps led down to the water. At the water's edge there were some wider steps and a small floating wooden dock, but no beach. This was it. The villa was more like a cliff dwelling. I later learned that this was the way to get to and from the water from inside the villa, which was actually on the other side of the cliff. It was the perfect setting for both privacy and security. From that point on, part of our daily routine usually included a visit to "the Rock."

One day we were out in the boats, just drifting. It might have been the day Mrs. Kennedy took Caroline waterskiing. I'm not sure. It was calm, and the water was smooth and so clear that it looked like you could reach down and touch the bottom some thirty-five feet below. Mrs. Kennedy, Caroline, Princess Lee, Anthony, SA Hill, and I were all in the same boat together, and our skipper was standing in the front of the boat, facing us but not looking at us. He was looking over the side of the boat, very intensely, concentrating on something. Suddenly he dove overboard while the rest of us waited and wondered.

When he resurfaced, he climbed back on board and resumed his post in the front of the boat. Only this time he stood with his right arm extended over his head, holding a small squid like a trophy he had just won. Then, just as suddenly as he had gone overboard, he took the squid's head, placed it in his mouth, and bit down. He continued to stand there, proud and tall, the squid's black ink oozing out of the corners of his mouth, running down and dripping off his chin while the rest of us stared in horror. Luciano Grando, who was drifting beside us in another boat, quickly explained that in Italy squid head was considered a delicacy and what our skipper had accomplished was a rare feat. With our new understanding of the event, we all clapped appreciatively.

Another time, when we were returning to Amalfi from Conca dei Marini, the boats stopped, and again we started drifting. Apparently someone decided it would be a good idea to take a last-minute dip before we reached shore. So, everyone went overboard—Mrs. Kennedy, Princess Lee, and Caroline and Anthony with their little inner tubes. Clint and I intently watched for intruders from the Rivas, but no one bothered them while they played around laughing and splashing each other.

When they were finished, everyone but Caroline got back into the boats. She continued paddling around in her inner tube and told her mother that she wanted to swim to shore. Mrs. Kennedy agreed to her daughter's request, but someone had to go along with her. I knew that someone was going to be me. *Uh oh*, I thought, glancing toward the Amalfi shore and its pebble beach, which was about a quarter of a mile away, farther than I wanted to swim. Nevertheless, I slid into the water and watched as both boats slowly pulled away and headed for shore.

Caroline was already paddling toward shore when I started my slow breaststroke to join her. At least Caroline had her little

Four-year-old Caroline Kennedy tries her
hand at steering a runabout off the Amalfi
Coast during Mrs. Kennedy's trip to
Ravello, Italy, August 1962. *Author's collection*

ducky inner tube, which made me feel more comfortable, and in
the back of my mind I jokingly toyed with the question of just
how much weight that little ducky could hold. We reached shore
safely, and Mrs. Kennedy was already there to greet us. Caroline
received a great big congratulatory hug from Mom for her efforts,
but there was no hug for me.

Our daily routine with Caroline and Anthony was soon established. Provi would appear in the morning with the two children
in tow. We would climb into the beach cars and head for the

fun drive down the mountain to Amalfi. In Amalfi we would pile into the Rivas and go to the villa in Conca dei Marini. We would hang out, maybe take a boat to the public beach, and then go back to the villa for a time, before returning to Ravello. In the evening Provi would take the children to Giardino Cantarini to play. It was here that Caroline made friends with a little Italian girl about the same age.

One morning there was an absolutely gorgeous yacht anchored in Amalfi's bay. It was far larger, more beautiful, and more distinctive than any other boat in sight. The yacht belonged to Gianni Agnelli. His father was president of the Fiat motor company, and Gianni was the chairman. *No wonder the Fiat connection,* I thought. I hoped he didn't peek at the car I had arrived in.

Agnelli and his wife, Marella, had arrived the previous evening and joined Mrs. Kennedy and her sister in Villa l'Episcopio. It appeared the Agnellis would be staying for a while, and their yacht, the *Agneta,* was available for their hosts' whims. It didn't take long for Mrs. Kennedy to take advantage of this offer, and soon everyone was off sailing the coast of the Tyrrhenian Sea— everyone except the kids, that is. I got to stay back with Caroline and Anthony, while Special Agent Hill was on board the *Agneta* and Special Agent Rundle followed in a police escort boat. Again I hummed to myself; this time it was "Red Sails in the Sunset." *What's with these musical themes that keep popping into my mind?* I wondered.

As their sojourns took them south to view the ancient Greek ruins of Paestum, where Allied troops had landed during World War II, and north to the island of Elba, where Napoleon was exiled, I continued the daily Caroline/Anthony routine, riding up and down the mountain and making use of the villa in Conca dei Marini. I wasn't complaining. Caroline was the reason I was in Southern Italy in the first place. What more could I ask for?

All special agents on our trip took turns doing night duty at
Villa l'Episcopio, and I actually looked forward to my turn. After
Mrs. Kennedy and the others retired, I would sit on the patio and
enjoy the peace and quiet of the night and the view, which in
its own way was just as beautiful as during the day. August was
a festive month in Europe. Many businesses closed, and several
villages celebrated with festivities of their own. As if it weren't
beautiful enough with lights sparkling over the mountainside,
fireworks from the various villages added to the scene.

One evening after dinner, Mrs. Kennedy informed SA Hill
that she and the others wanted to go to Positano. Evidently, this
was a village where nightlife flourished. It wasn't far, less than
twelve miles west of Amalfi, but still it took forty-five minutes
to get there because of the narrow, twisting road. Mirrors were
even placed at the sharp turns so that you could see if anyone
was coming from the other direction. It was a harrowing drive
in daylight, let alone at night. Clint needed extra help, and I
was one of the agents chosen to assist. All went well, and even
the paparazzi left Mrs. Kennedy alone. As we were leaving, one
of the photographers handed me a picture that he had taken
of Mrs. Kennedy and me upon our arrival. I have no idea how
he developed it so quickly, because we were not in Positano
that long. We made it back to Ravello before midnight without
incident, the worst part having been the drive along the narrow
highway in the dark.

When we were off duty, we ate at one of the many small
restaurants in Ravello, usually one with an open-air patio and a
view. After a good pasta dinner, we wandered the Piazza Duomo,
visiting different vendors, eating Italian ice, and searching for
signorine. One evening we met a group of five young ladies and
started talking, English versus Italian. The Italian girls were interested in learning all about America and what it was like to be a

Author's collection

Secret Service agent. We, the agents, were interested in *signorine*. It was a funny scene with a lot of laughing, pointing, and giggling between the girls, when one of them pointed at me and said, "*piccolo bambino.*"

"What does she mean?" I asked.

"Little baby," someone replied, and everyone laughed. I laughed right along with them, but talk about deflating my ego balloon with one little pinprick. That did it. I actually didn't mind, though. I was still proud to be the youngest agent there.

When we left Ravello, I had an ache in my heart. Everyone had been so kind and friendly that I felt like I was leaving family behind. I had many fond memories—again, I was one lucky SOB. I had been in Italy for twenty-six days, and it was time to go home. "*Grazie per i ricordi*," or "Thanks for the memories," as Bob Hope would have said.

8

LACE, THE CUBAN MISSILE CRISIS, AND THE LOSS OF PATRICK

M RS. KENNEDY, CAROLINE, and our entourage returned from Italy on September 1, 1962. We spent the night at the Carlyle Hotel in New York City. The next day we did not continue on to Washington as I thought we would. I had forgotten that it was Labor Day weekend, so instead of going to Washington, we headed to New-port, Rhode Island, where the president was enjoying a long week of sailing on the *Honey Fitz* and getting ready to watch the America's Cup races, which would kick off in Newport on September 15.

The First Family was reunited, and I spent the next thirty-nine days protecting Caroline and John-John in a routine similar to the one I'd followed in Newport and Hyannis Port the previous fall. On Tuesday, October 9, I returned to DC after having been away for sixty-five straight days.

It was around this time that SA Hill approached me to see if I would be interested in transferring to Mrs. Kennedy's detail and working as his assistant. For the past six and a half months he had been handling the responsibilities of her detail alone. He needed and wanted help.

I was surprised when he asked me, but if he had enough faith and confidence in me and my ability to handle the additional, more intense responsibilities associated with guarding the First Lady, I was all for it. Chief James Rowley, the head of the Secret Service under Kennedy, approved SA Hill's request, and on Wednesday, October 17, 1962, I was officially transferred to the First Lady Detail—also known as the Lace Detail, after Mrs. Kennedy's code name. *Hot damn!* I thought.

There was something special about working with Clint Hill. His personality made him stand out from others. There was an air of confidence about him—how he carried himself, always alert and in control yet seemingly relaxed. There was good chemistry between the two of us, and we worked well together from the very start. Clint, having been with Mrs. Kennedy since day one, knew her habits, her likes and dislikes, and he passed them along to me. His advice gave me an enormous advantage for "getting along." The fact that I had also been around Mrs. Kennedy on the Kiddie Detail didn't hurt.

My new assignment to assist Clint could not have come at a more appropriate time, because events were about to get dicey. On October 14, 1962, a US U-2 spy plane flying over Cuba took several pictures showing Soviet nuclear missile sites under construction. President Kennedy received the pictures two days later, and thirteen days of tense top-secret negotiations followed between the president and Soviet premier Nikita Khrushchev before a settlement was reached regarding their removal. Those thirteen days became known as the Cuban Missile Crisis, and it has been said to be the closest we have ever come to World War III. Clint would have had his hands full if he'd had to go it alone.

We were given many instructions during this time, but the only specific details that stand out were the preparations for a possible evacuation of the White House. Agents were called to assemble on the South Lawn, where three helicopters had landed; we congregated near the middle helicopter, helicopter #2. Helicopter #1 was located closest to the Oval Office. It was for the president and his immediate staff. Helicopter #2 was in the middle. It was for the First Lady, Caroline, John Jr., and any staff or Secret Service agents assigned to them. Clint and I were the agents assigned to helicopter #2.

I remember ASAIC Roy Kellerman giving us our instructions. He told us to expect people to panic and try to push their way onto our helicopter. Our job was to ensure that *no one*—other than assigned personnel—got on board. He asked the assembled group if there were any questions.

I spoke up and asked, "What are we supposed to do if someone unassigned does try to board the helicopter?"

Looking me straight in the eye, ASAIC Kellerman instructed, "Shoot them and worry about the consequences afterward." There were no more questions.

I knew my job, and I knew what I had to do. We were reminded that evacuation plans were top secret and not to be discussed with anyone. Fortunately, tensions cooled and a settlement was reached, and there was never any need to evacuate the White House. I never had to shoot anyone.

After the crisis was averted, things went back to normal— normal for Mrs. Kennedy, that is. I continued the weekend trips to Middleburg, only now I was in the company of adults. The lease on Glen Ora was expiring, so I accompanied SA Hill when Mrs. Kennedy visited various farms and other locations in the area looking for a property where she could build.

Mrs. Kennedy also loved antiquing and was always searching for new acquisitions. Sometimes the president traveled with
Mrs. Kennedy, and at other times she traveled on her own. Other
travels included regular trips to the Washington School of Ballet
for Caroline's ballet lessons, and visits to theaters in Washington and New York City. We spent the Thanksgiving holiday in
Hyannis Port and Christmas in Palm Beach.

I never worried much about missing holidays with my family,
because I loved my work. That Thanksgiving I ate my turkey
dinner at the commissary at Naval Station Newport. Christmas
in Palm Beach was a change from the cold Ohio winters of my
childhood. The first Christmas, all the agents received an Izod polo
shirt and a photograph of the White House taken from the South
Lawn as gifts from the Kennedys. The following two years, each
agent received a large envelope with the presidential seal. Inside
was a color lithograph of a room in the White House. I still have
my copies of the Green Room and Red Room lithographs and
the photograph. The polo shirt is long gone.

―――――――――――

On Saturday, December 29, 1962, the president and Mrs. Kennedy
boarded a presidential helicopter and flew from Palm Beach to the
Orange Bowl in Miami. They were not going to attend a football
game. The president was greeting an assembly of recently released
Cuban exiles who had been held as prisoners by Fidel Castro,
prime minister of Cuba.

In 1959, during President Eisenhower's administration, Fidel
Castro came into power in Cuba after leading a military revolt
against Cuba's dictator, Fulgencio Batista. Under Castro's leader-
ship, Cuba embraced Communism, and our Central Intelligence
Agency didn't like the idea of a Communist state so close to

our borders. The CIA came up with a plan to oust Castro by
secretly training a group of Cuban exiles known as Brigade 2506.
They were to invade Cuba from its south shores at the Bay of
Pigs. President Kennedy inherited the plan with his inauguration
in 1961, and after less than three months in office he ordered the
invasion to begin.

The invasion was a flop. Several exiles were killed, and approximately eleven hundred members of Brigade 2506 surrendered.
They were held as prisoners for nearly twenty months while the
United States negotiated for their release. Now the surviving
members of Brigade 2506 were gathered at the Orange Bowl to
present President Kennedy with their flag.

I left Palm Beach at 7:30 AM with a group of agents who drove
to Miami to help with advance security at the Orange Bowl.
Clint arrived on the chopper with the president and First Lady,
and I joined him at Mrs. Kennedy's side during the president's
brief speech. Mrs. Kennedy then spoke briefly, in Spanish, and
both she and the president received a huge roar from the mostly
Spanish-speaking crowd. We had a white Lincoln convertible
there to drive the president and Mrs. Kennedy out of the stadium
to their waiting helicopter. I was told to cover the left rear of the
car, where I walked and jogged as we departed the Orange Bowl.
This was my first OJT experience covering a moving vehicle in
which both the president and the First Lady were riding.

Two weeks after returning to Washington from Palm Beach, Clint
and I were at Glen Ora farm in Middleburg with Mrs. Kennedy.
This was when Mrs. Kennedy told Clint that she was pregnant
and would be limiting her activities for the next few months.
Clint told me that this was private information and was to be kept

confidential. Only a few people already knew. Mrs. Kennedy always communicated directly with Clint, and he kept me in the loop.

The week after Mrs. Kennedy told Clint that she would be slowing down, she took a ten-day whirlwind trip to New York City with Caroline. While Mrs. Kennedy stayed in the Kennedy suite at the Carlyle Hotel, Caroline stayed with her two cousins Stephen and William Smith, who lived on Park Avenue just a short distance away. The Kiddie Detail was with us to help cover Caroline, and later in the week the president joined us. We spent a full ten days attending Broadway shows, dining in fancy restaurants, and visiting Central Park and the children's zoo, the United Nations Building, and the US Mission. Mrs. Kennedy also spent a lot of time antiquing on Madison Avenue.

After returning to DC, I had two days off. I was already nearing two hundred hours in overtime for the year and realized that for Mrs. Kennedy the phrase "limiting activities" didn't necessarily mean slowing down.

Over the next four months, Clint and I were kept busy. Since the lease on Glen Ora had expired and the new house near Middleburg, Virginia, was still under construction, Camp David, Maryland, became the venue of choice for weekend retreats. Camp David could not have been more perfect. I was familiar with it from my days assigned to President Eisenhower's grandchildren in Gettysburg. It was a presidential retreat located in the Catoctin Mountains of Maryland, about sixty miles north of Washington. Operated by the US Navy, it was surrounded with double chain-linked fencing topped with barbed wire and patrolled by marines with guard dogs. Security was definitely not a concern.

We made two more holiday trips to Palm Beach, one for Washington's Birthday and one for Easter. We went on three more antiquing trips to New York City. We made helicopter trips to and from Camp David and the new home's construction site in Atoka, Virginia, and of course we still had all the normal daily activities in Washington, even after Mrs. Kennedy's pregnancy was made public in mid-April.

By the end of June, we were back on Cape Cod, only this year the president and Mrs. Kennedy rented a different house. Brambletyde was located on Squaw Island at the end of Squaw Island Road, a little farther away from the Kennedy Compound than we had been the previous summer but still within walking distance of a mile or so. The White House Communications Agency, the newly created successor to the White House Army Signal Agency, had provided a trailer/office/command center by the entrance to the property, and that's where we hung out when we weren't busy.

The month of July proved to be very quiet and uneventful, except for weekends when the president and his entourage of staff and agents arrived. Then there would be a burst of activity for a couple of days, and after the president left, things would quiet down again.

Mrs. Kennedy's daily activities were limited to Squaw Island and the immediate vicinity. One day she took Caroline and John Jr. clamming in a marsh that was located behind Brambletyde. She had them in a punt, a small, flat-bottomed boat, and was pulling them along by a rope, while she waded in knee-deep water feeling for clams buried in the muck with her bare feet and toes. For the entire month of July, she had only attended one riding lesson with Caroline. That was on July 11, and that's why I was surprised on the morning of August 7 when Mrs. Kennedy emerged from Brambletyde, holding Caroline's hand, and told me she was going to the Allen Farm with Caroline for her riding lesson.

I was expecting another quiet day hanging around Squaw Island, but a break in the routine sounded good. Clint had taken the day off, so it was me and the Kiddie Detail. Mrs. Kennedy and Caroline entered the car that I was driving, and off we went to Osterville and the Allen Farm. Special Agent Lynn Meredith from the Kiddie Detail followed us in a separate car.

When we reached the farm, Mrs. Kennedy immediately went to the front porch of the farmhouse and sat down in a chair while SA Meredith and I walked to the stable with Caroline. Once mounted on Macaroni, Caroline headed for the paddock with her trainer. The paddock was located between the house and stable, so Mrs. Kennedy had a full view of Caroline from where she sat, and SA Meredith and I leaned against the outside of the fence surrounding the riding ring.

We had been standing watching the lesson for fifteen or twenty minutes when Mrs. Kennedy stood up and started walking toward us. She approached me and whispered, "Mr. Landis, I think we had better leave now, but I want Caroline to stay and finish her riding lesson. Can we sort of sneak off so she doesn't notice and start making a fuss?"

"Yes, ma'am," I replied—like I'm going to say *no* to the First Lady! I turned to SA Meredith and clued him in to what was happening, and then Mrs. Kennedy and I headed to the car.

I opened the rear door to the car for her, and as she slowly slid in she said, "Mr. Landis, can we please hurry?"

Being the alert and intuitive agent that I was, I sensed a tone of urgency in her voice, so I jumped in behind the steering wheel and immediately floored it, throwing gravel helter-skelter. No, what I actually did was ease the car onto the highway and, while driving slowly through traffic and the center of town, got on the radio and called the command center at Squaw Island.

Ensign George Dalton answered my call. *Thank goodness*, I thought, feeling relieved. If anything needed to be done, Ensign Dalton was the man who could do it.

"George," I said into the microphone, "It's Paul. I'm in Osterville with Mrs. Kennedy. We just left the Allen Farm and are headed back to Squaw. I think she's going into labor. Call Dr. Walsh and tell him to get there immediately, *and* get hold of Clint and tell him to get there ASAP. It's an emergency. Call and have a helicopter on standby too."

We made it through town and traffic and had mostly clear sailing ahead of us. We had ten miles to go, and the road was narrow and windy, with little hills and dips that could leave your stomach in your throat, like riding on a roller coaster. I was driving as fast as I dared, clutching the steering wheel in both hands when I wasn't on the radio and only slowing down for the curves. Meanwhile Mrs. Kennedy was sitting in the backseat talking to me in her familiar whispery, husky voice: "Mr. Landis, can you please go faster? Go faster. Please!"

All of this was happening and I was thinking to myself, among other things, *Please, Mrs. Kennedy, please hang in there. Please don't have this baby now, not on my watch.* I knew we had facilities set up at Otis Air Force Base for just such a situation. The problem now was getting there. So, there I was, a bachelor, the youngest agent on the protection detail, alone, in a car racing down a country road at eighty miles per hour with the First Lady of the United States in the backseat, and she was having labor pains. *I could soon be in a rather intimate situation with the First Lady,* I thought. *God help us both.*

I had not received any instructions on what to do in this type of situation, and I definitely had not received any OJT. However, I did remember reading something once in a "How to Survive in an Emergency" book about what to do if you were in a car with a pregnant lady and she went into labor. You were supposed to immediately stop the car, have the woman get in the backseat, and while placing her feet against the back of the front seat, push along with the contractions.

Yeah, right. Like I'm supposed to hold the First Lady's hand and count while the two of us take deep breaths together and count: one, two, three—*push*, or go huff-huff-huff—*push*. I certainly didn't want this to happen, but if it came to it I would definitely stop the car, cross my fingers, call for help, and hope for the best.

The only section of road that I was actually concerned about was a quarter-mile stretch by Craigville Beach where it was a flat straightaway. The speed limit there was only ten miles per hour because of pedestrian traffic between the beach and the parking lot, and there were big speed bumps that could really jolt us. It was still too early for beach bathers, but when we reached the area, I had to slow down anyway, regardless of how Mrs. Kennedy felt. As I eased through the area, I didn't hear a word. There was nothing but silence.

We were almost there. I made the final turn onto Squaw Island Road, and with less than a mile to go I saw a military helicopter approaching and descending toward Brambletyde. I pulled to a stop in front of the communications trailer just as the helicopter's wheels touched down, and a car carrying Dr. John Walsh, Mrs. Kennedy's obstetrician, pulled up and stopped beside us.

"Perfect," I almost shouted. The timing was perfect.

I jumped out from behind the steering wheel and opened the car door for Mrs. Kennedy. I was helping her out when Dr. Walsh came up, took her by the arm, and led her up the front steps and into the house. *We're home free*, I thought.

A moment later, Dr. Walsh and Mrs. Kennedy came back outside. With a tone of urgency in his voice, Dr. Walsh said, "We need to get to Otis, *immediately*."

Clint, what about Clint? Where the hell is Clint? I turned to Ensign Dalton and told him, "Call Clint and find out where he is. Tell him we're on our way to Otis."

Dr. Walsh and Mrs. Kennedy were already aboard the helicopter, and the chopper's engines were revving up. I hurriedly climbed on board, and by the time I was buckled in, it was wheels up. I looked out the window, watched Brambletyde grow smaller and smaller as we distanced ourselves, and wondered what had happened to Clint and what lay ahead for me.

It only took about ten minutes to fly to Otis AFB, and by the time we landed and the helicopter door opened, Clint was there to greet us. *He made it*, I thought. *Whew!* I knew how much Mrs. Kennedy depended on him. Finally, maybe I could relax— just a little bit.

Clint accompanied Dr. Walsh and the First Lady to an emergency surgical room while I secured a ten-room emergency wing and waited for any news.

At 12:52 PM, August 7, 1963, Patrick Bouvier Kennedy was delivered by Cesarean section. He was premature and was having difficulty breathing. He was immediately placed in an incubator and wheeled into my area. I peeked into the incubator. I had never seen a baby so tiny and frail looking. He appeared so small that you could probably hold him in the palm of one hand. I was told to keep a close eye out and to allow NO UNAUTHORIZED PERSON into the area, and that meant NO ONE.

There was a constant buzz of activity for the next four hours, and the time passed by quickly. President Kennedy arrived and was constantly in and out of the recovery room where Mrs. Kennedy was supposedly resting. The base chaplain, Father John Scahill, arrived to baptize Patrick. Everyone paced and waited while doctors consulted. The doctors eventually determined that Patrick was afflicted with hyaline membrane disease (HMD), or respiratory distress syndrome (RDS), a fairly common respiratory problem found in prematurely born children due to insufficient lung development. The emergency facilities at Otis were not equipped to handle this type of emergency, so it was decided that Patrick had to be rushed to Boston Children's Hospital for proper treatment. *Another emergency*, I thought.

I was selected to accompany Patrick to Boston. His incubator was loaded into the back of an ambulance, and a small medical team joined us. I got into the front seat and sat beside the driver. At 5:55 PM we departed Otis AFB, accompanied by a full police escort with lights flashing all the way to Boston, but without sirens. At 7:17 PM we reached Children's Hospital, where medical staff and special agents from the Boston Field Office greeted us. Security was already established on Patrick's floor, so I sat and waited.

President Kennedy arrived at some point, bringing his own contingent of agents. We now had Secret Service agents from the President's Detail, plus agents from the Boston Field Office, swarming all over the place. I was beginning to feel a little self-conscious, because all the other agents were in a suit and tie and I was in the same clothes that I had started the day with, plus I was getting a little stinky. My mission was accomplished, and I felt like a fifth wheel. I needed to get back to Hyannis Port where I belonged, with the First Lady and Clint.

But there was a problem. The ambulance that I had arrived in was long gone. I was stranded without transportation. Finally, at 12:10 AM, one of the special agents from the Boston Field Office was assigned to drive me back to Hyannis Port, where I was able to pick up an official car of my own and end my shift at 3:00 AM.

I reported back for duty at 1:00 PM that same day and worked until midnight. There was no news from Boston, and in a way, that was good news. However, when I showed up at 7:00 AM the following morning, Friday, August 9, Clint was somber. He informed me that Patrick had died nearly three hours earlier, at 4:04 AM. *After all we had done*, I thought. *Damn!*

9

GREECE

MRS. KENNEDY RETURNED to Brambletyde a week after Patrick's death and spent the remainder of August resting and recuperating on Squaw Island. President Kennedy arrived on the weekends, as usual, and over a long Labor Day weekend the president and First Lady spent a lot of time cruising around Narragansett Bay on the *Honey Fitz*, while SA Hill and I spent a lot of time in the jet boats keeping sightseers away.

On September 12 our activities shifted to Newport and Hammersmith Farm, where the president and First Lady celebrated their tenth wedding anniversary. Their good friends Ben and Tony Bradlee joined them for a week of swimming, sailing, and partying. On September 17 the First Lady even joined the president and the Bradlees in a round of golf at the Newport Country Club. This time I got to walk along with the foursome, not like my previous golf course experiences. It was the first and only time I ever saw Mrs. Kennedy swing a golf club. She was a little awkward but didn't do too badly. Everyone laughed and teased each other a lot, making it fun to watch. It was obvious that the First Lady was feeling better, and I figured we were heading back into our previous seasonal travel routine. However, maybe there was another reason the First Lady was so happy.

When Clint told me, I thought he might be teasing. I don't remember exactly when it was, but one day he had this twinkle in his eyes and an expression on his face like *I know something you don't know.* He said, "Guess what's up? Guess where we're going?"

"I haven't the faintest," I replied, thinking DC or Palm Beach.

"Greece," Clint said.

"Greece," I replied. "You mean the country Greece? No way. When?"

"Next month. Nothing definite yet. Maybe early October. In the meantime, I have to bust my butt to make arrangements and get SA Ken Giannoules over there for the advance."

SA Giannoules was our Greek-speaking agent, and he had been to Greece with Clint in the spring of 1961, when Mrs. Kennedy and Princess Lee visited Athens. This was when I was still assigned to Glen Ora farm in Middleburg.

And then Clint announced, "And oh, by the way, we will be sailing on Aristotle Onassis's yacht the *Christina.*"

Apparently, this all came about during Princess Lee's visit to Hyannis Port after Patrick's death and was followed up through long-distance communications and planning between the First Lady and her sister after Princess Lee returned to Europe. Princess Lee was acquainted with Greek shipping magnate Aristotle Onassis, and she had told him that she thought her sister needed and deserved a little R&R after losing Patrick. Onassis offered the use of his yacht if the two of them decided they wanted to visit Greece together. The *Christina,* named after Onassis's daughter, was thought to be the fanciest private yacht in the world. How could the First Lady resist such an opportunity? The problem was convincing the president.

Onassis had some previous criminal issues with the US government dating back to the end of World War II, when he purchased fourteen surplus ships from the US Maritime Commission and violated the terms of his purchase agreement. *Plus* he was known as a jet-setter. There was an upcoming presidential election in 1964 to consider. How would all this look to the public? The president agreed to the trip, but only if Prince Stas Radziwill, Princess Lee's husband, went along, as well as another couple acting as chaperones. The president selected his friend Franklin D. Roosevelt Jr. and his wife, Suzanne, for the task.

On Monday, September 23, 1963, our Newport visit ended with a helicopter flight from Hammersmith Farm to Quonset Point Naval Air Station, where we boarded Air Force One for our return to the White House via Andrews Air Force Base outside DC.

Mrs. Kennedy had started a school in the White House for Caroline and a few of her close friends. On the first day, September 25, she had arranged for a field trip to Dulles International Airport and a ride on the Goodyear Blimp. Clint was tied up making arrangements for Greece, so I accompanied Mrs. Kennedy and the children to Dulles along with the Kiddie Detail. All my recent thoughts had been about sailing on the sea on board the *Christina*, but today my thoughts were about sailing through the air in a blimp.

It was not meant to be. Seating capacity on the blimp was limited, and Mrs. Kennedy and the children had first priority for the ride, so I was grounded. Instead, one of the Kiddie Detail special agents acted as security for the group. I stayed and worried until everyone returned.

Finally, Tuesday, October 1, arrived—it was departure day for Greece! Clint and I would work a regular day before leaving for New York City to catch an evening flight. Emperor Haile Selassie of Ethiopia arrived in Washington that morning by train. He was in the United States for a week-long state visit, and the president and First Lady went to Union Station to greet him. After all the hoopla and speeches, a short motorcade followed to the

Blair House, the residence just across the street from the White House where the emperor would be staying. But the First Lady skipped out on the motorcade and did not ride in the limousine with the president or the emperor. We returned to the White House, where I assumed that Mrs. Kennedy was making final preparations for our trip.

At 8:25 PM, we departed Washington National Airport via Kennedy's private plane, the *Caroline*, headed to Idlewild International Airport in New York City. Then at 9:45 PM Mrs. Kennedy, her personal assistant Provi, Clint Hill, and I boarded Trans World Airlines flight 840, en route to Athens, Greece, with a stopover in Rome.

Clint had reserved first-class seating for Mrs. Kennedy, Provi, and himself. As for me, he reserved an aisle seat in the first row behind the bulkhead in economy. While they flew in comfort, I catnapped and prevented anyone from entering their private space. Do you think I cared about being in the economy section? Are you kidding me? I was on my way to Greece. This was not like taking a trip with the president, where it was stop and go and stop and go, staying nowhere for any length of time. I was on my way to a two-week cruise of the Greek Isles on board the most fabulous yacht in the world.

After eight hours of a semi-sleepless night, we landed in Rome. We deplaned and spent an hour in TWA's VIP lounge while local passengers flying to Athens boarded our plane. Then the four of us reboarded for the final leg of our flight, and two and a half hours later we landed in Athens. Princess Lee and Prince Radziwill were there to greet us along with a small welcoming party. After hugs and handshakes and all the other required formalities were over, we left and drove to a nearby villa in Kavouri owned by Markos Nomikos, one of Aristotle Onassis's friends and also a shipping tycoon. Kavouri was about twelve miles from Athens.

Clint had already visited this exact same location with Mrs. Kennedy and her sister on a previous visit in the spring of 1961, so he knew the layout. After everyone was settled in for the day, I was finally off duty at 6:00 PM.

When I woke up the following morning, I knew where I was, but it took me a few moments to sort through all my hours, overnights, and time changes to figure out what day of the week it was. After figuring out that it was Thursday, October 3, I reported for work with Clint.

We spent our first full day in Greece visiting various Greco-Roman ruins like the Acropolis and the Parthenon. I saw so many columns of ancient temples that I don't remember what was what. In the evening and that night, everyone just hung out at Nomikos's villa. I stayed on duty past midnight, knocking off at 1:00 AM.

Mrs. Kennedy visits the Theatre of Dionysus at the Acropolis, Athens, Greece, with FDR Jr. and his wife, Suzanne (front left), October 3 or 4, 1963. *Author's collection*

Eight hours later I was back on duty. Soon after, we departed for Piraeus, the harbor of Athens, where the *Christina* was anchored. I was eager to see what all the fuss was about over this fairy-tale floating paradise.

When we reached Piraeus and I looked out over the bay, I noticed one anchored yacht that stood out from all the rest. It was by far the largest yacht there. *That's got to be it*, I thought, and I soon got confirmation. It was the *Christina*, and it was 325 feet long—longer than a football field. Wow! Aristotle Onassis had provided two Chris-Craft-type speedboats to shuttle us from shore. The boats were already waiting for us when we arrived. After we were ferried to the *Christina* and welcomed aboard, the speedboats were lifted and stored on board too.

I had no idea who else was on board or in our welcoming party, other than recognizing Onassis from his pictures and the ship's captain by his uniform. Provi, Clint, and I were just necessary tagalongs. Anyway, Clint had the manifest, and he would clue me in later. I wanted to check out the yacht.

This is what I learned and saw during the course of our cruise. In addition to at least two speedboats, there was a small sailboat aboard. There was also a small twin-engine seaplane with a crew member pilot who made daily business and mail runs to and from Athens. The big deal was to wait for his announced return, when everyone would come on deck and watch him land in the water after buzzing the yacht, upside down. The plane was then hoisted on board until the next day's flight. The whole process of lowering and lifting the plane was fascinating to watch.

There were nine staterooms, each one named after a Greek island, and each one lavishly furnished with gold and brass fixtures and expensive works of art. I was disappointed that Clint and I were not offered the use of one of these fancy staterooms.

The seaplane approaches the *Christina*. *Author's collection*

However, as I said, we were just uninvited tagalongs and had to settle for a cabin below deck along with the rest of the commoners and crew. Our closet-sized "stateroom" was much smaller and a tight fit for the two of us. It was furnished with a small sink, a teeny-tiny closet, and two bunk beds. Being the junior agent, I got the top bunk. We did have our own toilet and shower, however, which was an appreciated bonus.

Don't get me wrong—I'm not complaining. Not at all! Clint and I were there for one reason and for one reason alone: to ensure the safety of our country's First Lady to the best of our abilities. That was our top priority. Lucky for us, it just happened to be on board the most famous yacht in the world.

But wait, there was still more to see. On the aft deck was a minotaur-themed mosaic tile dance floor that could be filled with seawater and converted into a swimming pool in a matter of minutes. There was a small bar that made a big impression: the barstools were covered with whale foreskin, which was a leather quite soft to the touch. The footrests and armrests were made from whale ivory, and the armrests were scrimshawed with the adventures of Achilles, including his siege of Troy and the kidnapping of Helen, the most beautiful woman in the world. (In retrospect, I wonder if there was a hidden message in the decor.) There was a comfortable library, where the bookshelves were filled with leather-bound copies of Greek classics, and if that wasn't enough, it contained a fireplace with a mantel made from the deep blue semiprecious gemstone lapis lazuli. The other thing I remember is a beautiful spiral staircase that ran between three decks; I learned that the handrail was made from black onyx, another semiprecious stone. Even the white marble used aboard came from the same marble quarry used to build the Parthenon in 447 BC.

There was a doctor's office, a movie theater, a beauty salon with two hairstylists, a masseuse, a laundry and dry cleaner, and a galley with two chefs—one French, one German. The crew of sixty even included a band.

It was hard to believe that this world-famous yacht was once a WWII antisubmarine frigate destined for the scrapyard. Onassis bought it for $34,000 in 1954 and then proceeded to spend an additional $4 million to convert it into a floating palace. Why? I guess because he could.

When I joined the United States Secret Service in 1959 seeking adventure, never in my wildest dreams could I have imagined that I would experience something like this. I was one lucky fella.

Clint and I happened to be leaning on the starboard railing when the launch with Franklin and Suzanne Roosevelt arrived, and the two of us watched as they boarded the *Christina*. FDR Jr. was the undersecretary of commerce, and he had been to Egypt and Somalia prior to joining us in Piraeus. Mrs. Kennedy's chaperones had arrived. Let the party begin, and it did.

Clint had me stand by while he went to the bridge to befriend the captain and possibly talk to Onassis. This trip was about as laid-back as it could be, and we needed to know where we were going so that some advance security precautions could be established. We had our advance agent SA Giannoules on shore, and Clint could contact him from one of the forty-two onboard telephones. This was going to be a real wingding, touch-and-go type of operation, and we needed to know our destinations as far in advance as possible.

When Clint returned, he said, "Istanbul. Destination Istanbul, Turkey." *So much for the Greek Isles*, I thought, and Clint and I both knew we'd better be on our toes. Onassis could be sneaky, and this trip might be full of surprises. Clint had some phone calls to make.

That evening Onassis threw a welcoming dinner party for Mrs. Kennedy, while Clint and I ate below deck with a few of the ship's crew. I don't remember what was served, but I knew that the two of us were not going to starve to death on this cruise. At 11:38 PM the *Christina* weighed anchor and slowly eased into the Aegean Sea. I remained on duty and out of sight until 4:00 AM, spending most of my time on the bridge or in the pilot house. I was ready to hit the sack.

Later that same morning I awoke to the sound of silence. There were no engines droning and there was no sense of movement like there had been when I fell asleep. I was due back on duty at noon anyway, so I got up, got dressed, and went topside to see what was happening. We were anchored in a bay offshore from a small village on the island of Lesbos, the third-largest Greek island in the Aegean Sea. There was a monastery overlooking the village from the top of an extinct volcano. It had rained recently, and the sky was still overcast. In spite of the cloud cover, it was all quite picturesque with the mountain in the background, the

red tile roofs of the village, the white sandy beach, and the clear
blue water of the bay. There was a sense of expectation in the air.

"We're going exploring," Clint said. "Grab your gear. Everyone
is going, except for Onassis, that is. He's remaining on board the
Christina."

We visited a few shops in the village, but the monastery seemed
to be the main event, and the only way to reach it was by foot
up a rather narrow, steep, rocky trail. As we made the climb,
everything seemed kind of surreal to me. The air was still damp
and misty from the rain, vegetation was sparse, and the sky was
overcast with different shades of gray and black clouds. The gray
stone monastery looming above only added to the scene. I felt
like I was in a 1930s black-and-white horror movie. We all made
it to the top, and I wondered, *What next? Are we expected? Will
we be invited inside? Do we have an appointment? Or is someone
going to knock on the door and when it opens say, "Hi, we just
happened to be passing by and wondered if . . ."*?

That was not the case, however, and Dr. Frankenstein was not
there to greet us. Expected or not, we were greeted with a warm
welcome from a polite monk, and everyone was invited inside. We
received a complete tour of the monastery and learned much about
its history and the remote lifestyle of its occupants. It was impressive but definitely not a lifestyle that I could embrace. There was
too much out there to see and do, and I wanted to see and do it all.

After our monastery visit, we hiked back down the mountain
and returned to the awaiting *Christina*. The sun was out, and we
soon resumed our journey to Istanbul. We continued across the
Aegean Sea, northeast to the Dardanelles, a narrow strait (one to
four miles wide, forty-two miles long) that ran through Turkey
and connected the Aegean to the Sea of Marmara.

As we neared Istanbul, a launch approached and pulled alongside the *Christina*. It was for Clint. He rode it ashore to make

security arrangements for our visit. I stayed on board the *Christina* with Mrs. Kennedy, and we continued to cruise on through the Bosporus Strait into the Black Sea and back. When we returned at 10:55 AM, Clint was ready and waiting.

I escorted Mrs. Kennedy ashore, where Clint had arranged for transportation, and we all headed off to the famous Blue Mosque, a top priority and one of the reasons for our visit. We also went to Topkapı Palace Museum, and I got to see a solid-gold throne that I had heard about. It was much smaller than I had envisioned, and it didn't look too comfortable to sit in, but it was still quite impressive, with inlaid emeralds and rubies the size of my fist.

When our Istanbul visit ended, everyone reboarded the *Christina*, and at 7:04 PM we headed back south through the Aegean Sea toward Crete. Crete is the largest of the Greek islands and separates the Aegean Sea from the Mediterranean.

Sometime during this part of the cruise, Clint approached me. He had an expression on his face like that of the cat that swallowed the canary.

"What's up?" I asked.

"Morocco," he calmly replied, smiling.

"What do you mean Morocco?" I said.

"I mean Morocco," he said again. "Marrakech, Morocco. We are going to Marrakech, Morocco."

"When?"

"Right after our cruise, directly from Athens to Marrakech. King Hassan is sending a private plane to pick us up."

I wondered if Marrakech was anything like Casablanca—"Here's looking at you, kid" or "Of all the gin joints in all the towns in all the world, she walks into mine." Visions of palaces and veiled dancers entered my head. Thoughts of the French Foreign Legion, which I had once actually considered joining when thinking about romance and adventure, briefly entered my mind.

"Meantime, I've got to get hold of Giannoules and get him over there, ASAP," Clint said. "And don't say anything. No one else knows." I had learned by this point that I was not the youngest agent on the White House Detail; SA Ken Giannoules had me beat by a couple of months. However, I still looked the youngest.

I had thirty-eight hours to fantasize about Morocco before we finally anchored off the coast of Heraklion, the capital city of Crete. Mrs. Kennedy wanted to visit some ruins in nearby Knossos, so again Clint went on shore ahead of us to arrange for transportation. We were only there for about five hours before heading off again—this time, destination Ithaca.

Ithaca is a small island located off the western coast of Greece in the Ionian Sea. I remembered Ithaca from my humanities courses in college: it was the supposed home of Odysseus, the Greek hero in Homer's *Odyssey*. I ought to remember. I had to take Humanities twice in order to graduate.

I don't remember going ashore at Ithaca, but I think this is where we had an incident that could have been disastrous. In any case, this is what happened. It was a dark and moonless night, and sometime after dinner, Clint and I happened to be on deck watching the crew lower one of the speedboats into the water.

Clint turned to me and said, "I wonder what's going on? I'd better check it out." But before he had a chance, everyone came out of the dining room and started heading down a ladder into the speedboat. This was unannounced and came as a complete surprise. Clint and I followed, hustling down the ladder and jumping on board. All seats in the speedboat were occupied, so Clint and I had to fit onto a small deck area located behind the backseats. We just had time to grab on to whatever we could find when the driver hit the throttle and we were off, full speed ahead.

Clint and I looked at each other, both of us thinking, *How sneaky. Nice try, Ari, but no way were you going to ditch us.* I was hanging on with all my strength, as I assumed Clint was too. None of us were wearing life jackets. It was dark, really dark, and we were running full throttle without running lights. I didn't see a light anywhere ahead, to the side, or behind us. Even the *Christina* had been left somewhere behind and was out of sight in the dark. I was also thinking this was not too smart, not smart at all, and dangerous, but the situation was completely out of our control.

Everyone in the boat was laughing and having a gay old time, everyone except for Clint and me. We had been speeding along for quite some time when for some reason the driver finally decided to turn on a spotlight. I do not know what prompted him to do so at that particular moment, but when he did, all I saw was a sheer rock cliff looming straight ahead. We were heading full throttle directly into a cliff! I thought we were all goners.

Immediately a headline followed by all sorts of rescue and survival thoughts flashed through my mind: FIRST LADY GOES MISSING ON GREEK CRUISE. Please let me survive. Where is Mrs. Kennedy? Locate Mrs. Kennedy. Find wreckage or rocks to cling to. Find Clint. Is he OK? If anyone else survives, keep priorities straight. Mrs. Kennedy first, then check on Clint. Everyone else is on their own.

There wasn't time to slow down, but the driver reacted quickly enough, cutting the steering wheel sharply all the way to the left. Thank God I didn't get thrown off. The boat swerved past the cliff so close I felt I could have reached out and touched the stone with my bare hand. That was a close call—too close. Everyone in the boat was still laughing. I don't think they realized how close we all had come to being killed.

Well, I didn't think it was so funny. I was glad to be back on board the *Christina* after our little joyride, and I thought that was all it was. But that wasn't the end of Onassis's little tricks.

The following morning, we weighed anchor at 5:10 AM and headed toward Skorpios, a small island just a short two-hour cruise north of Ithaca. What was so special about Skorpios? It was Onassis's island. He actually owned an entire island. We spent the rest of the morning walking around Skorpios, and by noon it was back on board the *Christina* and time to weigh anchor again.

We headed east through the Gulf of Patras toward Drepano. Drepano is a city located along the northern shore of the Greek Peloponnese in the strait that separates the Gulf of Patras from the Gulf of Corinth and mainland Greece from the Peloponnese.

My daily records for this trip are still in my possession. We were moving from place to place, and I believe we were actually anchored by Patras, a city and port located nearby, just south along the coast of the Peloponnese. This is when Onassis's next attempt at trickery took place.

There were some sites in Patras that Onassis wanted to show to Mrs. Kennedy and the rest of his guests. As we had previously done, Clint made the necessary calls and went to shore to make final arrangements while I stayed on board the *Christina* with the First Lady. We were probably anchored no more than a hundred yards offshore, and I could see Clint in the distance. When cars and drivers were ready, Mrs. Kennedy and I boarded our runabout, only this time Onassis himself took the helm.

We started out motoring directly toward Clint and the waiting cars. However, when we were about halfway there, Onassis made a sudden sharp turn to the right and opened up on the throttle. *You SOB*, I thought, and started waving my hands frantically overhead pointing in the direction that we were going. I saw Clint and a driver jump into a car, and the race was on. As we sped along the shoreline on the water, I watched Clint's car speed along the coast on land. Anyone watching probably wondered what the hell was going on, right along with Clint and me.

By the time Onassis finally slowed down and turned toward shore, I had lost sight of Clint behind some buildings. I wondered what had happened, where he was, and what I was going to do. Onassis docked the boat, and we started walking up some steps over a slight embankment leading to the street level. When we reached the top of the steps, there was Clint, standing next to a limo, door wide open, and wearing a huge smile on his face. I almost burst out laughing. That's your Secret Service in action!

Clint's timing could not have been more perfect. He had saved the day. Onassis, however, did not look too pleased with the end result. After a brief tour and visit, we again boarded the *Christina*, and I remained on duty until midnight. I fell asleep that night thinking how we had beaten Onassis at his own game. How sweet it was. Clint's recollection of the location and what happened differs slightly from mine, but the story is essentially the same.

It was time to head back to Athens. We cruised all night, all the following day, and the following night, arriving in Athens at 11:00 PM on Saturday, October 12. Our cruise had come to an end, and what an adventure it had been. This kid from Worthington, Ohio, had seen places he never imagined possible.

Our final night in Greece was spent on board the *Christina*. In the morning it was time to pack up and say good-bye. I felt sad to leave, and why not? For twelve days, I had experienced the lifestyle of the rich and famous. I had memories that I would never forget. But it was time to move on to the next adventure. We had a flight to Morocco to catch.

———————

Our chartered aircraft was ready and waiting when we arrived at the Athens airport. It was a French Sud Caravelle, a short- to medium-range jet-propelled passenger plane that could carry up to a hundred people. Medium-range jet airliners were relatively new on the scene in 1963, with most jet passenger planes built for long-range flights. The plane belonged to Royal Moroccan Airlines and came with a full crew. I thought this was a big deal, since there were only five of us: Mrs. Kennedy, Princess Lee, Provi, Clint, and myself. I could hardly believe we had an entire airplane to ourselves. I tried sleeping during our three-and-half-hour flight but was unsuccessful. I kept thinking about my past two weeks, about where I had been, and now, about where I was going. Morocco was going to be a real change from the *Christina*.

When we landed in Marrakech, I did not know what to expect. The movies I had seen about Morocco conjured up visions of camels. There were no camels, just the usual welcoming party and lineup of cars and drivers. I don't remember if King Hassan was there or not, but I figure he had to be. After all, when he had visited the White House in April, he had personally extended the invitation for Mrs. Kennedy to visit.

We had about a three-mile drive into the city to the king's Bahia Palace, which was located inside the orange-red clay wall that surrounded Marrakech. I had seen pictures of the wall in movies and magazines, but this was the real thing. I learned that the protective wall ran twelve miles completely around Marrakech, and up to nineteen feet high in places, with twenty gates and two hundred towers. Passing through the gate gave me goosebumps. I was entering into a strange and foreign environment.

When we arrived at the Bahia Palace, Mrs. Kennedy, Princess Lee, and Provi went inside, but Clint and I were stopped at the door. The palace guards were quite emphatic about not letting us enter, so much so that we didn't press the issue. This did not present a problem security-wise, but if the two of us were responsible for Mrs. Kennedy's safety, what were we supposed to do? It wasn't so much that we were worried as it was a matter of protocol—we had to know what was going on.

Clint stepped up and demonstrated how he had earned his code name Dazzle. He was a smooth talker and managed to romance his way into the palace. When he came back outside, he was smiling and told me we were all set and that all issues were resolved. Everything would be the same as if we were at the White House when Mrs. Kennedy was in the private quarters, but if Mrs. Kennedy was going out, we would know when and where in advance. For this we depended on Provi. She always knew what was happening and was able to give us a heads-up. Once everything was squared away, the two of us were shown to our accommodations, which were separate but still attached to the main palace.

Our room had once been the home of concubines who were part of a king's harem. The walls of the room were mostly painted white but had mosaic tile everywhere—on the floor, on the archways, even on the ceiling. Heavy wooden doors opened onto a courtyard, but I don't remember any windows, just openings in the walls for air circulation. The only thing missing were ladies dancing around in gauze pantaloons with veils covering their faces. *Geez, I hope I'm able to get some rest*, I thought as I fantasized. We were in a whole different world.

There were two dressers for clothes, and on top of each dresser was a sixteen-ounce bottle of Pour Un Homme cologne. I had never seen such a large bottle of cologne and never heard of Pour Un Homme. It smelled good but was quite strong, and after I learned about the water situation and bathing habits in Morocco, I understood why. As a desert country where water was often scarce, it had somewhat different hygiene customs from those I was accustomed to in the United States. During the entire trip I was appalled at the open sewage ditches outside the walls. I also wondered about import rights for Pour Un Homme in the United States, because I had never heard of it before and thought it might be a good investment opportunity.

Our visit happened to coincide with the celebration of the birth of King Hassan's first son, Prince Mohammed. He had been born in August, so why wait until October to celebrate, I wondered. I learned it was a Moroccan custom to keep an open grave for forty days after a child's birth, until the health of the mother and baby is ensured. After learning this, I wondered how Mrs. Kennedy felt, having lost Patrick only two months earlier, but she showed no open signs of grief.

Berber tribes and hundreds of Berber tribesmen from the surrounding mountain and desert communities poured into Marrakech to celebrate. It was a free party, and they came to participate in the festivities and camp outside the walls. On our first day, King Hassan and an entourage of followers escorted Mrs. Kennedy outside the city's walls to observe a part of the Berber celebrations. The terrain was flat, lacked vegetation, and was dusty. There were tents everywhere. The king had his own private tent, and the ground inside the tent was covered with beautiful rugs piled on top of one another to keep down the dust and provide comfortable footing. I personally found them difficult to walk on, and I couldn't believe that such beautiful rugs were just scattered around on the earth. I wondered how they ever cleaned them.

Berber tribesmen were not well known for their literary acumen, but they were known to be fearless fighters, and what they lacked in literacy they made up for in skilled horsemanship. One part of the festivities that we witnessed was a series of competitions that pitted two tribesmen against one another in a sprint on horseback and ended with both men firing their black powder rifles either into the air or at the ground, the object being to fire their weapons at the exact same time, making one big bang and creating one huge plume of white smoke. Of course, this never happened exactly as it was supposed to, so another pair of tribesmen would repeat the act, and the end result would be the same.

This went on all day long, one race after another. It was exciting to watch as the tribesmen charged, approaching from the distance, weapons held high in one hand above their turbans. In the other hand they held the reins, djellabas flapping in the breeze, dust flying from the thundering hooves, and the sound of trilling tongues rising to a high pitch as the horses approached. One could not help but get caught up in the thrill of the race.

After feeling comfortable enough that no rifles were going to be pointed in our direction, I decided that this was definitely picture worthy, especially if I could capture both rifles discharging at the same time. The tribesmen always discharged their rifles in front of our tent, probably to impress King Hassan, because I doubt that they even knew who Mrs. Kennedy was. I thought that it would make a better picture if I could capture them head on, so I walked onto the field in between races and waited for the next two riders. I had my Kodak Motormatic 35, Kodak's first 35 mm auto exposure camera. I stood and waited. Finally, the signal for the next race was given, so I raised the camera to my eye and peered through the viewfinder. No "Caution, images may be closer than they appear" warning appeared, like the message on today's rearview mirrors, so I just stood there waiting as the horses came closer and closer. I could hear the trilling of tongues rising to a high pitch as the tribesmen approached, racing side by side. When I decided they were getting close enough and about to fire their rifles, I started snapping away. *Kaboom*, I got it!

I lowered my camera, but there was no place to go. The horses were there, right on top of me. If I moved an inch, I would be trampled. I froze and held my breath. One of the tribesmen was

Author's collection

staring right at me with piercing dark eyes, almost daring me to move. Both horses brushed my sides as they passed. *That was too close for comfort*, I thought, my heart racing a mile a minute. *What a stupid stunt!* I was supposed to be watching out for Mrs. Kennedy's safety, not jeopardizing mine. I wouldn't be much good in the hospital.

When I returned to the sidelines, Mrs. Kennedy was laughing and said in her familiar wispy voice, "Oh, Mr. Landis." Clint asked me if I needed to go back to the room for a change of underwear.

Most of Mrs. Kennedy's three and a half days in Marrakech were spent visiting various palaces, where Clint and I were denied entry. We were never comfortable with it but got used to it. It was a situation that called for diplomacy, not overassertiveness. Clint had been in this kind of situation before, and he handled it well. After all, we were guests in a foreign country and they had their own rules to abide by, no different than if King Hassan was visiting the White House in DC. We would not allow his protective personnel to wander around in the private quarters, either. When Mrs. Kennedy was inside, all Clint and I could do was keep our fingers crossed.

We left Marrakech on October 17, 1963, by the same way we arrived: Royal Moroccan Airlines charter jet. I could get used to this kind of travel, but reality returned after we arrived in Paris and transferred to Pan American Airways flight 119, heading for home. Seating arrangements were the same as when we departed Idlewild Airport in New York sixteen days earlier. I was behind the bulkhead in the economy section, while everyone else was in first class.

At some point during our trip home, Mrs. Kennedy spoke to Clint about a trip the president was planning to take to Texas. The president wanted her to go with him, but Mrs. Kennedy was on the fence about the trip. Eventually she decided to accompany him, so Clint and I would be headed to Texas too. Our departure was set for November 21, 1963.

10

TEXAS

THE PAN AMERICAN flight home from Greece and Morocco was quiet and uneventful. It gave me time to reflect on the previous two and a half weeks, and also time to think about the upcoming trip to Texas. I had just completed one fantastic adventure and was about to begin another.

The Texas trip would be my first OJT trip of a political nature. I was looking forward to a new learning experience. Whoever said "If you love your job, you will never work a day in your life" certainly hit the nail on the head. I felt like I hadn't worked a day yet since joining the Secret Service just over four years earlier.

When our Pan Am flight arrived at Idlewild Airport, Captain Howard Baird was there waiting for us with the *Caroline*, ready to fly us back to Andrews AFB. When we arrived at Andrews, the president came on board to welcome Mrs. Kennedy home. Mrs. Kennedy was still seated in the middle of the plane, and the president walked down the aisle, bent over, and gave her a kiss. I happened to be seated three or four rows behind Mrs. Kennedy, and to be silly, I put on a souvenir fez that I had purchased from a kiosk in the Marrakech market. I also put on a big smile. When the president looked back and saw me, he didn't smile. He just shook his head from side to side and said, "Off with the fez, Mr. Landis."

Needless to say, the fez came off and immediately went into my flight bag. At the time, I didn't think about any possible political implications if the press happened to take pictures of me in the fez while we were departing the *Caroline*. I was just trying to be funny. I was sorry to see our trip end, but after seventeen straight days of travel, it also felt good to be back home.

Clint and I were home for less than two full days before we were off to Camp David with the First Lady, Caroline, John Jr., Maud Shaw, and the Kiddie Detail. It was a weekend filled with quality time for Mrs. Kennedy and the children. When we all left Camp David on October 20, 1963, little did I know it would be my last visit.

The next four weeks flew by quickly. Mrs. Kennedy and the children now spent their long weekends at the new house in Atoka, Virginia. Caroline's pony Macaroni, as well as Mrs. Kennedy's horse Sardar, had been transported into their new stable, and a new updated office/command post was provided for the Secret Service. Mrs. Kennedy also hired the same caretaker and housekeeper couple from Glen Ora farm, David Lloyd and his wife, Catherine, so there were some familiar faces.

Most children John Jr.'s age had a sandbox to play in or swing to play on, but not John-John. He had his own real airplane. It was the body of a decommissioned US Army or Air Force Piper Cub–style military trainer. Of course, it was minus its wings and engine, but the rest of the plane was intact. Someone had it placed in the woods near our Secret Service office. John Jr. loved playing in it, and what kid wouldn't?

Mrs. Kennedy was back into her weekend routine, only now the weekend destination was Atoka. She would leave the White House by helicopter with the children on Friday afternoons, and President Kennedy would join them on Saturday, also arriving by helicopter. Then on Monday everyone would leave Atoka and return to the

White House by helicopter. I usually drove one of the official cars back and forth with some members of the Kiddie Detail.

On Tuesday, November 19, 1963, I drove one of those official cars from Atoka back to the White House before knocking off for the day. It was supposed to have been my day off. The next day, Wednesday, was also supposed to be a day off, but I had to report to the White House at noon for a final briefing on the Texas trip. I wasn't upset; having to work on a day off was nothing new to me. It just came with the job. I was used to it.

Everyone who attended the briefing received a schedule of all of the planned activities for the next two days, Thursday, November 21, and Friday, November 22. I still have this schedule in my possession. Everything on it is detailed from the minute the president was scheduled to leave the White House at 10:45 AM on Thursday morning through Friday afternoon, when we were scheduled to arrive at Vice President Lyndon Johnson's ranch at 10:20 PM in Austin. I also received a detailed itinerary of what was planned for every location, including the exact dress code and the number of expected attendees. Most important to me, I received an assignment sheet that detailed my duties at each location.

Following the distribution of our assignment sheets, we all received a briefing on the general negative mood in Texas, with the main focus on Dallas. I learned that Dallas had become known as the City of Hate. This was all news to me, because I had always thought of Dallas as a pretty cool place, and I was looking forward to seeing it in person. Dallas was "oil country," home of the "big rich." Oil baron H. L. Hunt had offices there. It was also the home of the original Neiman Marcus, the famous department store. This trip was going to be a pretty big deal for me.

SCHEDULE

THURSDAY - November 21, 1963

√10:45 a.m.	Depart White House - helicopter
√11:00 a.m.	Depart Andrews AFB - jet
√1:30 p.m.	Arrive San Antonio International Airport
√1:40 p.m.	Depart airport - car
√2:25 p.m.	Arrive Aero-Space Medical Health Center
√2:30 p.m.	Dedication program starts
√3:00 p.m.	Program over.
√3:05 p.m.	Depart Aero-Space Medical Health Center - car
√3:25 p.m.	Arrive Kelly AFB
√3:30 p.m.	Depart Kelly AFB - jet
√4:10 p.m.	Arrive Houston International Airport
√4:15 p.m.	Arrive Houston International Airport
√5:00 p.m.	Arrive Rice Hotel
√6:20 p.m.	Drop-in at dinner-dance in Rice Hotel, sponsored by League of United Latin-American Citizens
√8:35 p.m.	Depart Rice Hotel - car
√8:45 p.m.	Arrive Coliseum - Congressman Albert Thomas Dinner
√9:30 p.m.	Depart Coliseum - car
√9:55 p.m.	Arrive Houston International Airport
√10:00 p.m.	Depart airport
√10:45 p.m.	Arrive Forth Worth - Carswell AFB
√10:50 p.m.	Depart Carswell AFB - car
√11:10 p.m.	Arrive Texas Hotel - Room 919

FRIDAY - November 22, 1963

√8:45 a.m.	Attend breakfast in hotel sponsored by Forth Worth Chamber of Commerce
√9:45 a.m.	Breakfast over - return to room
√10:30 a.m.	Depart Texas Hotel - car
√11:05 a.m.	Arrive Carswell AFB
√11:15 a.m.	Depart Carswell AFB - jet
√11:35 a.m.	Arrive Dallas - Love Field
11:45 a.m.	Depart airport - car

12:30 p.m.	Arrive Trade Mart - Attend luncheon sponsored by the Dallas Citizens Council, the Dallas Assembly and the Graduate Research Center of the Southwest
2:00 p.m.	Depart Trade Mart - car
2:30 p.m.	Arrive Love Field
2:35 p.m.	Depart airport - jet
3:15 p.m.	Arrive Austin - Bergstrom AFB
3:30 p.m.	Depart Bergstrom AFB - car
3:55 p.m.	Arrive Commodore Perry Hotel
4:15 p.m.	Attend reception in hotel sponsored by Democratic State Committee
6:00 p.m.	Depart Commodore Perry Hotel - car
6:05 p.m.	Arrive governor's mansion - attend reception
6:45 p.m.	Depart governor's mansion - car
6:50 p.m.	Arrive Commodore Perry Hotel
8:15 p.m.	Depart Commodore Perry Hotel - car
8:20 p.m.	Arrive Municipal Auditorium
8:30 p.m.	Seated at head table - fund-raising dinner sponsored by Dem. State Comm.
8:45 p.m.	Program starts
9:15 p.m.	Program over
9:30 p.m.	Depart Municipal Auditorium - car
9:45 p.m.	Arrive Bergstrom AFB
9:50 p.m.	Depart Bergstrom AFB - helicopter
10:20 p.m.	Arrive Vice President Johnson's ranch

ATTACHMENT NO. 2 - POST ASSIGNMENTS

HOUSTON INTERNATIONAL AIRPORT - ARRIVAL

(1) Point where President deplanes — SAIC Bertram / SA Pontius
(2) Press Area — SA Berger / SA Ready / 2 - Detectives
(3) Roped Area for Public — SA Sulliman / SA Johnsen / SA Gleson / 50 Houston P.D. / 5 Detectives
(4) Reception Area — ATSAIC Stout / SA Hill

AIRPORT - DEPARTURE

(1) Roped Area for Public — SA Lawton / SA McIntyre / 50 Houston P.D. / 5 Detectives
(2) Press Area — SA Berger

RICE HOTEL - ARRIVAL

(1) Point where Presidential limousine stops (Main Street Entrance) — SA deFreese / 4 Detectives
(2) Press Areas — ATSAIC Roberts / SA Lawton / 2 Detectives
(3) Sidewalk opposite Entrance (Roped Area) — SA Berger / SA Ready / 40 Uniformed Officers
(5) Door to Presidential Suite (Check Point) (5th Floor) — SA Landis / 1 Detective
(6) West Hallway - 5th Floor (Check Point) — SA Bennett / 1 Uniformed Officer

RICE HOTEL - DEPARTURE

(1) Press Areas — SA Olsson / SA Wilson / 2 Detectives
(2) Lobby Area — SAIC Bertram / 12 Uniformed Officers / 2 Detectives

Attachment No. 2 - Post Assignments
Page two

Uniformed Officers, Detectives and Firemen of the City of Houston will be posted in and around the restricted areas, i.e. stair-landing, air-duct intakes, electrical units, kitchens, etc.

LULAC DINNER - RICE HOTEL

(1) Second Floor Lobby (Near elevators) — SAIC Bertram / 4 Uniformed Officers / 2 Detectives
(2) Entrance to Grand Ballroom — SA Johnsen / 2 Detectives / 2 Uniformed Officers
(3) Area near Bandstand — SA Sulliman / 4 Detectives / 2 Uniformed Officers (in rear)

Uniformed Police and Firemen of the City of Houston will be posted in the kitchen area, all exits, electric unit area, and all elevator landing areas.

COLISEUM

(1) Point where Presidential limousine stops — SA deFreese
(2) Press Area - Entrance — SA Landis / 4 Detectives
(3) Seated at Table to President's left — ATSAIC Roberts
(4) Seated at Table to President's right — SA Ready
(5) Waiting Room behind head table — SA Bennett relieved by SA Johnsen / 2 Detectives
(6) President's steps (center) to head table relieved by SA Berger / SA Hill / 1 Detective
(7) Steps (on President's left) at end of head table relieved by SA Lawton / SA Sulliman / 1 Detective
(8) Steps (on President's right) at end of head table relieved by SA McIntyre / SA Olsson / 1 Detective

Uniformed Officers, Detectives and Firemen of the City of Houston will be posted completely around the restricted areas including the main floor, electric power unit, air-conditioning units, all stair exits, ramps, aisles, etc.

Special Agent Paul Landis's schedule and assignment sheets for President Kennedy's Texas trip. Landis made notes and checked off events after they occurred. Note that the check marks stop upon arrival of Air Force One at Love Field. At this point Landis became occupied with the president and the First Lady as they transitioned to the motorcade through Dallas. *Author's collection*

We talked about UN ambassador Adlai Stevenson's visit a month earlier, when an unruly crowd spat on him and he barely got out, but hearing the part about calling our president a traitor and the United Nations a Communist front was foreign to me. In my mind the occurrence had just been a one-time incident. But at this time there was a lot of bad publicity coming out of Dallas regarding the president's visit. It was an awakening for me, and a reason to be on alert.

On Thursday morning, November 21, 1963, I reported for work at 9:00 AM and parked my Corvette in my regular parking spot on West Executive Avenue. Grabbing my suitcase and trusty flight bag, I headed for the side entrance to the West Wing of the White House. When I reached the West Wing lobby, I was immediately directed to the South Portico, where I left my suitcase for the motor pool. I wouldn't see it again until the end of the day at the Hotel Texas in Fort Worth. I kept my flight bag with me and returned to the West Wing lobby to wait.

The West Wing lobby was abuzz with positive energy. Members of the presidential staff, the White House press corps, and special agents were hustling back and forth checking up on last-minute arrangements and details for our trip. I went into our Secret Service office off the lobby to do the same.

There were no last-minute changes to my duties. I was still assigned to the press plane, a chartered Pan American 707 jet, AF 6970, scheduled to depart Andrews AFB at 10:30 AM, half an hour ahead of the president. I would be driven to Andrews along with ATSAIC Emory Roberts, leaving the White House at 9:45 AM. I checked my watch and noted that I still had a few minutes before my scheduled departure. I wandered back out into the lobby, spotted Clint, and joined him. Clint was flying on Air Force One (AF 26000) with the president and Mrs. Kennedy. We would join up at each of our stops throughout the day.

About that time, SA "Muggsy" O'Leary wandered over. I assumed that Muggsy got his nickname because his teeth were missing and his toothless "mug" made it so that he just kind of gummed his words when he talked. I never knew this to be a fact, but one thing I knew for sure was that, besides being a really nice person, Special Agent John J. "Muggsy" O'Leary was someone special.

Muggsy was a former member of the Washington, DC, police department and had been with the Capitol Police when President Kennedy was still a senator. President Kennedy trusted him completely, and when the president moved into the White House, Muggsy came along as part of the deal. At the president's "suggestion," Muggsy became a special agent.

At first, several agents resented Muggsy, because he hadn't come up through the ranks or had any special training. However, that resentment soon dissipated once they learned that Muggsy wasn't such a bad guy after all—*plus*, he was a direct pipeline to President Kennedy. If you needed to know something, you just asked Muggsy and he would find out, bypassing the supposed chain of command.

Clint had to leave, but Muggsy and I stayed and talked about the trip. I told him how excited I was to be going on my first campaign event when Muggsy said, "You ain't seen nothin' yet. Wait until you see this political machine really go into action." He reached into one of his bulging suit jacket pockets and pulled out a bundle of gold tie clips wrapped in brown tissue paper. The clips were in the shape of PT-109, the patrol boat President Kennedy had commanded heroically as a naval lieutenant in WWII. Muggsy handed them to me while reaching into his other jacket pocket and pulling out another bundle. He said, "Hand these out sparingly," and then reached into a pants pocket and pulled out a third small package of gold chain bracelets with a small round

PT-109 pendant on a blue enamel background. "Be very discreet with these," he said. "They're expensive."

Our conversation was cut short when I got the high sign that my ride was ready to leave. I put the three bundles into my flight bag, thanked Muggsy, and was off to Andrews AFB with the rest of the agents who were leaving in advance of the president. I never had the opportunity to pass out those souvenir pins and bracelets and still have most of them secured in my local bank's safe deposit box.

Our flight departed Andrews AFB at 10:30 AM eastern standard time and arrived at San Antonio International Airport at 12:55 PM central standard time. It had been a three-hour-and-twenty-five-minute flight, and we landed thirty-five minutes ahead of Air Force One. That gave me enough time to deplane and familiarize myself with the setup on the ground. The president's limo, code name SS-100-X, and the Secret Service follow-up car, SS-679-X, or "Halfback," had been flown in ahead of time on a cargo plane from Washington, DC. The president's driver, SA Bill Greer, and follow-up driver, SA Sam Kinney, already had the two cars staged in place. SS-100-X had started out as a midnight-blue 1961 Lincoln Continental and was stretched and heavily modified to meet Secret Service requirements. Halfback was an eight-passenger 1956 Cadillac Series 75 presidential limousine.

Advance agents were at their assigned posts, and everyone was ready and waiting for the arrival of "Angel," the code name for Air Force One. An enthusiastic and friendly crowd had gathered behind a fenced-off area, and they were already chanting "Jackie! Jackie! Jackie!" They wanted to see the First Lady as much as, if not more than, the president.

Once Air Force One landed and taxied into place, a ramp was rolled up, and the stage was set. A welcoming party consisting of Vice President Johnson, his wife Lady Bird Johnson, Texas governor John Connally, and his wife Nellie, plus a bunch of other people I didn't know or recognize, were there waiting to greet the president and First Lady.

When the door to Air Force One opened, Mrs. Kennedy was the first person to appear. The crowd went absolutely wild, and louder shouts of "Jackie! Jackie!" filled the air. When President Kennedy appeared from behind her and stepped to her side, the noise level got even louder. The president and First Lady descended the ramp to the awaiting welcoming party, and that's when I spotted Clint and ASAIC Roy Kellerman deplaning behind them.

Once the welcoming ritual was completed, the president turned and headed toward the spectators. The crowd roared, and Mrs. Kennedy turned to follow the president. I joined Clint, who was at her side, and the two of us stayed with her, walking along as she followed the president, both of them waving and shaking hands.

After a few minutes of "campaigning," the motorcade was ready to depart. Everyone went to their assigned vehicles, and as the president and First Lady entered the president's limo, they were joined by Governor and Mrs. Connally. The motorcade departed for Brooks Air Force Base and the Aerospace Medical Center, where the president was to give a brief dedication speech. As they left, Clint jumped onto the left running board of Halfback, taking a position beside the driver, SA Sam Kinney. As much as I wanted to go along, my assignment was to stay with the two airplanes. I would see him again in Houston.

The San Antonio International Airport had been great for our arrival because of public access, something that would not have been available on a military base. (What good is a campaign trip if you aren't available for the public to see?) But now Air Force One and AF 6970 had to be moved to nearby Kelly Air Force Base, a mere fifteen miles south, where the president and First Lady would reboard after the president's dedication speech. I stayed on board AF 6970 while this transition took place.

At 3:55 PM, AF 6970 departed Kelly AFB for Houston, and a half hour later I was being driven to the Rice Hotel, where the president and First Lady would be making a brief stop. I was assigned to post #5, located outside the entrance to the $150-per-day fifth-floor International Suite, where they would be staying. A detective from the Houston Police Department was also there, so I had company and someone to talk to while we waited for President and Mrs. Kennedy's scheduled arrival at 5:00 PM. We found that the two of us had a lot in common. He was an avid outdoorsman and loved guns, golf, fishing, and hunting, all of which I enjoyed too. In fact, he told me that the first day of deer season actually started the very next day, Friday, November 22.

The Rice Hotel was an interim stop intended for the president and First Lady to use as a place to rest, relax, and freshen up in between the day's events and their evening activities. There were still two events to go before the end of the day. There was an 8:20 PM drop-in dinner/dance within the Rice Hotel, sponsored by the League of United Latin American Citizens (LULAC), followed by a 9:00 PM dinner honoring Congressman Albert Thomas at the Sam Houston Coliseum.

I did not assist Clint at the LULAC drop-in. Instead, at 7:15 PM, I went ahead to the Coliseum with ATSAIC Emory Roberts and six other agents (SAs Ready, Lawton, McIntyre, Bennett, Goodenough, and Berger), where I was assigned to the Coliseum press area entrance. Along with four detectives, I checked IDs and press passes.

After the dinner I rejoined ATSAIC Roberts and his crew, and we were transported to Houston International Airport, where I boarded AF 6970 for the fourth time that day. We departed

Houston at 10:20 PM and forty-three minutes later touched down at Carswell Air Force Base on the outskirts of Fort Worth. I was then transported to the Hotel Texas in downtown Fort Worth, where I again awaited the arrival of the president and First Lady and Clint.

When we arrived at the hotel, I could hardly believe what I was seeing. It had rained, and there were puddles of water in the street, but even so, the area in front of the hotel was jammed with people of all ages. Young adults, older adults, teenagers, parents holding toddlers on their shoulders—you name it, they were all there. The inclement weather plus it being a school night didn't matter. The crowd was so loud and enthusiastic and friendly that it gave a final energy boost to the day.

The decibel level grew even louder when the president and Mrs. Kennedy finally arrived. The magic that this couple inspired is unimaginable today. *What a perfect ending to a long and busy day*, I thought. I rejoined Clint and ASAIC Kellerman as they escorted President and Mrs. Kennedy to their suite on the eighth floor of the Hotel Texas, room 805. It was midnight, and I knocked off duty for the day.

The Secret Service had a temporary security office set up elsewhere on the eighth floor (room 862), and that's where Clint and I were told we would find our luggage. We picked up our suitcases and took them up to the ninth floor, where we were sharing a room for the night (room 944).

I was still hyped up from the size of the crowd and the greeting we had received in front of the hotel, too wide awake and too hungry to sleep. I headed out into the hallway looking for someone to go down to the lobby with me in search of a press room and some free food. I asked some agents who were milling about if they wanted to come along, but most of them just wanted to go to their rooms, call their wives, and crash. Clint still had a couple of things to do but said he would meet me in the lobby when he was finished.

Four or five other agents beat me to the punch and were already in the lobby by the time I got there, plus there were a couple of members of the press corps whom I didn't know. They were debating what to do, because there was no press room in our hotel. Merriman Smith, a senior member of United Press International (UPI), showed up just as Clint arrived and mentioned that the Fort Worth Press Club was nearby and we could probably get something to eat there.

"Let's go," I said, and out the door we all went.

By the time we arrived at the club, the dining room was almost empty. *Where is everyone?* I wondered. *Why aren't they here loading up on free food?* To our right, rows of tables were lined up with telephones and typewriters on top, but the chairs were askew and empty. The room appeared exactly as I imagined a newsroom would look like, minus the newsies. Only two men in white dress shirts with their sleeves rolled up were there, working on cameras or some sort of technical equipment. Then it dawned on me that it was after midnight Texas time, a little late to be scrounging around for free food. No matter; we were still hungry.

A long table covered with a white tablecloth was in the center of the room. This is where a buffet was served. Now there was no food, nada, not even a crumb. Only dirty dishes, empty beer bottles, and a few empty drinking glasses remained. An improvised bar was still set up, and a few stragglers were still hanging around. At least we were able to finagle a drink. I had a scotch and soda but was still hungry. Someone out of the remaining group of stragglers or workers mentioned a place called the Cellar—a beatnik joint that stayed open all night where we could probably get something to eat. It was located only a couple blocks away from our hotel. Two or three of our group opted out and decided to return to the hotel, but not me. I was still hungry, plus I wanted to see what a "beatnik joint" was really all about.

The Cellar was nothing special, but it was appropriately named. It was just a bar in a basement, but it was open and it served food. It was quite dark, and even as my eyes slowly adjusted to the dim light, a haze of cigarette smoke made it difficult to see. We spotted and surrounded an empty table, and a waitress dressed like a Playboy Bunny, minus the rabbit ears, came over to take our order. I ordered a scotch and soda and a hamburger and fries.

"Sorry, the bar's closed," she replied. "They shut down the bar at 1:00 AM." Either by bad timing or good fortune, we had just missed the last call.

How on earth did it get to be after 1:00 AM? No wonder the Press Club was nearly empty. All the press had already put in a full day's work and were in bed. As for me, even after a long day, I was still wide awake.

The waitress suggested trying a "salty dick," a house specialty, and that's what I remember it was really called. It was nonalcoholic and made with grapefruit juice and something else, I don't remember what. Feeling adventurous and game, I had a couple. There was a ring of salt around the rim of the glass. I'm guessing it was like a "salty dog" minus the alcohol. They tasted pretty bad. When my burger came, I ordered a Coke.

There were some other agents there who had arrived before us, but by the time we arrived most of them were just getting ready to leave. A few lingered on and joined us, along with some local detectives who happened to have covered the day's activities. Everyone was exchanging war stories and talking about cases they had worked on or arrests they had made, and I completely lost track of time. Guys slowly filtered back to the hotel, but I stayed and talked until the wee hours of the morning.

Before I knew it, we were asked to leave. I looked at my watch. It was 4:00 AM central standard time. The bar had to close for one hour before it could reopen again at 5:00. Contrary to published statements regarding the events that took place that night at the Cellar, I was not personally drunk nor did I witness any Secret Service agents who were drunk or misbehaving in any manner whatsoever.

Back at the hotel, I went to my room to lie down for a couple of hours of rest, but I couldn't sleep. I couldn't believe that I still felt wide awake. I was thinking about the day ahead and wondering what it was going to be like. I was going to be in my first motorcade, and in my mind, I was rehearsing what I had been trained to do in Secret Service School. I wondered if the agents who had stayed in their rooms all night were also having a sleepless night.

I finally got up, showered and dressed, and went down to the hotel's coffee shop for some breakfast. After breakfast, I saw ASAIC Roy Kellerman in the hotel lobby. He waved me over, and I immediately thought that I was going to be chastised for staying out late. It was now 8:00 AM. Instead, he said, "Paul, get outside and see ATSAIC Roberts. There's a large crowd out there, and the president has decided to give an impromptu speech. I need all the help I can get, and I need it now."

I was surprised, because the schedule I had received at our briefing two days earlier indicated that the first event on Friday, November 22, 1963, was to occur at 8:45 AM: "Attend breakfast in hotel sponsored by Fort Worth Chamber of Commerce." I didn't think Mrs. Kennedy even planned to attend that, so I'd thought that I would have plenty of time before I had to meet Clint outside the Presidential Suite. But Kellerman needed help, and I was available.

It had rained again since I was last outside earlier in the morning. Now it was drizzling lightly, and at first it appeared like it was going to be a dreary gray day. However, a few bright spots were starting to appear between the clouds. *Maybe this is going to turn out to be a beautiful sunny day after all.*

A flatbed trailer had been set up in front of the hotel. I didn't remember seeing it when we arrived the previous night. It could have been there and I just missed it because it was dark and I was too intent on the cheering crowd located behind some barricades in front of me, or it could have been set up earlier this morning. Either way, it was there now and held a podium with some steps leading up to it.

There were lots of people outside in front of the hotel, just like when we arrived the night before, only you could see the size of the crowd more clearly in the daylight. Tons of people, all waiting, all hoping to get a glimpse of the president and First Lady. I don't know how anyone could judge the size of that crowd. The way they were jammed together it would be like trying to count the number of jelly beans in a gallon jug. All you could do was just take a wild guess. No wonder the president had decided to give an impromptu speech—voters were waiting. I had no idea how everything got pulled together on such short notice, but that wasn't my concern. I had to locate ATSAIC Roberts.

After I reported to Roberts, he assigned me to a position beside the steps leading up to the podium on the truck's flatbed. It wasn't long before President Kennedy emerged from the hotel. He was flanked by Vice President Johnson, Governor Connally, Texas senator Ralph Yarborough, and a couple of others whom I didn't know or recognize. The crowd went wild. It was unbelievable to see the welcome that this man commanded. There was no apparent animosity in Fort Worth.

After his speech, the president descended the steps, and without even a glance my way, he held out his right hand with the rolled-up speech and headed straight into the crowd. I took the speech, spotted ASAIC Kellerman, gave it to him, and followed the president. After the president finished shaking hands and performing his magic, I escorted him back into the hotel along with the rest of the agents.

The president was now running late for his scheduled breakfast in the Grand Ballroom, so while the president was hustled off to the event, I headed for the elevator and took it to the eighth floor to join Clint, who was waiting outside the Presidential Suite.

Prior to my reaching the eighth floor, Clint had received a message from President Kennedy requesting—or, should I say, *insisting*—on Mrs. Kennedy's presence at the breakfast. This was not the original plan; however, Clint had already relayed the message to Mrs. Kennedy and was waiting for her appearance outside the Presidential Suite. Clint told me to wait by the elevator, and when the First Lady emerged from suite 805, the two of us escorted her down to the Grand Ballroom breakfast.

When Mrs. Kennedy entered the Grand Ballroom, the entire room went crazy. She was greeted with a thunderous applause as everyone stood clapping and cheering. The cheering continued until the First Lady took her place at the head table on the dais. After the audience finally quieted down, the president spoke up and said, "Two years ago . . . I introduced myself in Paris by saying I was the man who had accompanied Mrs. Kennedy to Paris. I'm getting somewhat that same sensation as I travel around Texas. Nobody wonders what Lyndon and I wear." The audience roared.

Both the president and the First Lady were presented with Texas-themed gifts. Mrs. Kennedy received a pair of cowboy boots, and the president received a Stetson ten-gallon hat, which everyone was urging him to put on. I knew that the president was not big on hats, and I wondered how he was going to get out of this one. He managed somehow to graciously say something about putting it on after returning to the White House.

Following the breakfast ceremonies, the president and First Lady returned to room 805 while I waited in the hotel lobby with ATSAIC Emory Roberts and the day shift. It was about 11 AM, thirty minutes before my scheduled departure for Carswell Air Force Base and my flight to Dallas. I had packed my suitcase earlier and had already taken it to our security room, so that wasn't a worry. I would retrieve it at the end of the day in Austin.

While we all waited for the president and First Lady, ASAIC Kellerman was busy checking on weather conditions in Dallas. He was on the phone with the Dallas advance agent, SA Win Lawson. Dallas was only a thirty-three-mile, twenty-minute flight from Fort Worth, and weather conditions were about the same in both places. A decision had to be made regarding what to do with the bubble top of the president's limo. Do we put it on or leave it off? It took time to attach, and it would be nice to have it ready to go if needed. The bubble top provided great protection from the elements, but it also limited the public's view of the occupants, which was not good. Everyone knew how President Kennedy liked to be seen and appear open to the public. And this was a political trip, and every adult standing along the motorcade route was a potential vote.

The clouds in Fort Worth were starting to dissipate, yielding patches of blue sky. The same was happening at Love Field in Dallas, our destination point. The bad weather appeared to be moving out of the area. The final decision was to leave the bubble top off.

I did not have my assignment sheet for the day with me, so I left the hotel lobby and went outside to locate SA Bill Duncan, the advance agent for Fort Worth. President and Mrs. Kennedy were scheduled to motorcade from the hotel to Carswell AFB, where they would board Air Force One for the short flight to Dallas. I needed to know how I was going to get to Carswell. SA Duncan was standing by the lead car. "You're riding with me."

The motorcade left the Hotel Texas at 10:40 AM and arrived at Carswell AFB a half hour later. Air Force One and AF 6970 were both on the tarmac, jet engines whining and ready to go. I immediately headed for AF 6970, where I joined ATSAIC Stu Stout and his 4:00 PM–midnight shift. Once we landed at Love Field, they would go directly to the Dallas Trade Mart to handle security for a luncheon the president and First Lady planned to attend after the motorcade through downtown Dallas. I was to wait at Love Field for the arrival of Air Force One. Vice President and Mrs. Johnson were also flying on AF 6970, which gave it the designation Air Force Two. Once they came on board, with the VP Detail in tow, the door closed, the wheel chocks were removed, and we were off to Love Field. It was 11:20 AM central standard time.

Air Force Two arrived at Love Field less than five minutes ahead of Air Force One. There was another large crowd waiting to greet us behind a chain-link fence, and this crowd appeared to be at least twice the size of the crowd I'd just witnessed three hours earlier in front of the Hotel Texas. I deplaned and started looking for advance agent Win Lawson. Ten cars were neatly lined up for the motorcade, so I headed that way. Special Agent Sam Kinney was sitting in Halfback, our 1956 Cadillac convertible follow-up car. I jokingly asked him if he could tell me where the follow-up car was. He shook his head no and with his thumb he pointed over his shoulder. Then I saw SA Lawson standing by the right front fender of the president's limo, which was positioned in front of Halfback. I walked over to double-check that my assignment had not changed. Win assured me that nothing had changed. I was still assigned to the right rear running board of Halfback. I was good to go. I turned around and headed back to where we had landed less than five minutes earlier.

Air Force Two had already taxied out of the area, making room for Air Force One to be moored and staged at the exact same spot.

I heard the distinct sound of an approaching jet, turned to my right, and saw AF1 gliding in for a landing. I can still see in my mind today the sun reflecting off the special silver, blue, and white paint design, the presidential seal painted on its side appearing to glisten more than ever against the patches of blue sky and white clouds. *What a beautiful sight*, I thought, as shivers ran up and down my spine and my chest swelled with patriotism and pride. I had witnessed this same scene three times on the previous day, and each time I had the same reaction. It made me feel proud of my country, proud to be an American, and proud to be on the First Lady Detail in the Secret Service.

Air Force One taxied to a stop, and I moved up beside the exit ramp as it was rolled up and locked into place against the rear door of the plane. It was 11:40 AM. The welcoming party was in place. Vice President and Mrs. Johnson were standing beside the mayor of Dallas and his wife. Again, the president and First Lady emerged from Air Force One, and again the assembled crowd went wild as the two of them descended the ramp, followed by Governor and Mrs. Connally.

Everywhere we went it was the same. Large, friendly crowds greeted us, cheering and waving little American flags, with everyone hoping to get a close-up view of the president and especially of the First Lady. I was getting my own close-up view, too, only mine was an education in campaigning. I wondered if this was what the next few months would be like. I glanced around looking for Clint and saw him descending the ramp with ASAIC Kellerman. He joined our group and took a spot near Mrs. Kennedy's side.

Mrs. Kennedy received a bouquet of red roses, and a lady in a red coat handed President Kennedy a black leather picture frame containing two hand-drawn charcoal portraits, one of himself and one of the First Lady. After receiving this gift, President Kennedy turned and handed it to me and stopped briefly to speak to a lady in a wheelchair. He then turned and, with Mrs. Kennedy at his side, headed toward the cheering crowd that was being restrained behind the four-foot-high chain-link fence that separated the spectators from the welcoming area. Clint and I moved in closer as President and Mrs. Kennedy pushed through the mass of photographers, VIPs, and special guests who were assembled on our side of the fence. I realized then that I was still holding the leather picture frame, and this was not good. I needed to be hands free. I turned and gave the portraits to a familiar face, but today I can't remember who that was.

The Kennedys arriving at Love Field, Dallas, Texas, November 22, 1963. *Photo by Cecil W. Stoughton, National Archives, courtesy of Wikimedia Commons*

The president immediately started shaking hands, moving along the fence line from his right to his left. I was in front of him pushing my way through the photographers, clearing a path and keeping an eye on all the hands reaching over the fence, watching out for anything harmful or suspicious. Mrs. Kennedy had been walking beside the president, but I noticed that she was moving along slower and that she and Clint were becoming separated. I turned and asked another agent to move into my spot so that I could drop back and assist Clint.

Clint was positioned behind Mrs. Kennedy, so I slipped in front of her and continued clearing the pathway and removing an occasional obstacle. I reminded her to watch out for a curbing that ran along underneath the fence, so that she would not trip and fall. We reached a corner where the fence made a right angle turn to the left and someone was dangling a three-by-five-foot American flag in our path. I had to hold it up so that we could get by. A few feet farther, the fence made another right angle turn back in the direction we were originally headed.

At this point, Mrs. Kennedy stopped shaking hands and started to head toward the presidential limousine, which had been trailing along parallel but slightly behind us. When she didn't see the president, she stopped and asked Clint where he was, and he saw that the president was still walking along the fence, continuing to shake as many hands as possible. Mrs. Kennedy turned around and went back to do the same.

Finally, the president, realizing that he had a schedule to keep, turned away from the crowd and headed back toward the limo. I took up a position beside the limo and continued surveying the crowd while everyone was getting settled. Mrs. Kennedy entered the limo first and sat in the rear seat on the left, and the president sat beside her on the right. Mrs. Connally flicked down the jump seat in front of Mrs. Kennedy and sat there, while Governor Connally did the same thing and sat in front of the president.

The limousine began to move, and I followed along, half walking and half jogging. As our speed increased, I started to drop back to assume my assigned position on the right rear running board of Halfback, when suddenly I was pushed in the back and shoved aside. Dave Powers and Ken O'Donnell, both of them special assistants and longtime friends of President Kennedy, rushed past me, panting and half out of breath. The two of them jumped onto the running board of Halfback and climbed into the backseat area.

What the hell? Who did they think they were? My first thought was that they had no right to be in the Secret Service follow-up car; they would only be in the way, interfering with security. But what did I know? Politics had to be involved somehow, and that wasn't my bailiwick. This was my first motorcade, and I wasn't in a position to question or object. Plus, there wasn't time and this wasn't the place. We were on the move.

While recalling this moment, I would attempt to locate SA Win Lawson's original advance notes without success. Somehow, they seem to have disappeared. I wanted to know if Powers and O'Donnell were actually assigned to the follow-up car or if the two of them had just barged in. In September 2016, I visited the Sixth Floor Museum in Dallas and brought this subject up with its curator, Stephen Fagin. He told me that he knew of no record that existed that showed that this was their assignment, only that this was where the two of them were throughout the motorcade in Dallas.

At the time, however, I had an assignment and a job to do. Damned if I was going to be pushed aside and left behind because there wasn't room for me in the follow-up car. I jumped onto the running board and threw my left leg up and over, straddling the right rear door, half in and half out, knowing that I was secure in that position.

I remember seeing SA Don Lawton throwing up his arms, as if in frustration. He was part of ATSAIC Emory Roberts's detail, and he was being left behind. Why? I thought it was because of our uninvited guests, who took up so much valuable space that there wasn't room for him. I have since read that he was left behind to help secure the area for our departure later in the afternoon. I personally find this difficult to believe, because Love Field was already secured for our arrival. We were already short of agents and needed all of the on-site coverage we could get. Again, SA Lawton's original advance notes, if they were found, could either confirm or disallow my beliefs.

I remained in my same half-in, half-out position until we were leaving the airport area, when ATSAIC Roberts told me to resume my assigned position completely out on the running board. "Just in case," he said. It was 11:55 AM.

Dallas police chief Jesse Curry was driving the lead car, accompanied by advance agent Win Lawson, Dallas sheriff Bill Decker, and SAIC Forrest Sorrels from the Dallas Field Office. The president's limo came next, flanked by four Dallas Police motorcycle escorts, two on each side. SA Bill Greer was driving, and ASAIC Kellerman sat in the right front passenger seat.

Halfback, our open convertible follow-up car, came next. SA Sam Kinney was driving, and ATSAIC Emory Roberts, the shift leader, was in the right front passenger seat. In the rear seat, SA George Hickey sat on the left with an AR-15 rifle within easy reach at his feet. SA Glen Bennett, our protective research agent, sat on the right. The two intruders, Ken O'Donnell and Dave Powers, were in the middle on jump seats. Four of us were on the running boards. SA Hill was on the left front, SA Tim McIntyre on the left rear, SA Jack Ready on the right front, and I was stationed on the right rear.

We departed Love Field onto Cedar Springs Road to begin our ten-mile motorcade to the Dallas Trade Mart, where President Kennedy was due to speak at a luncheon sponsored by the Dallas Citizens Council. The lead car set the pace, and we were moving along at a fairly rapid clip for a motorcade, maybe thirty to thirty-five miles per hour. The highway was relatively void of spectators at this point, so there was no real reason to slow down. Besides, we were running behind schedule, and it provided an opportunity to regain a few precious lost seconds. That changed once we got closer to downtown Dallas.

The first part of the motorcade passed through a rather sparsely populated section of Dallas, typical of most major cities that I remember visiting in my travels. We passed an endless array of gas stations, drive-in restaurants, automotive repair shops, and used car lots. Most of the structures were only one or two stories high, and there were only a few people standing along the highway. The closer we got to downtown, the more the spectators began to line the sidewalks, one row at first, then two and three rows deep, with intersections the most heavily crowded. We passed a group of Cuban picketers holding up signs at one intersection, but I don't remember what they said other than CUBA. I was too busy concentrating on the people, not their signs.

A little farther along, closer to the main business district, some children had a sign asking the president to please stop and shake hands. The president's limo stopped, and when it did, a group of mostly children, but some adults, merged toward the car. I moved up and positioned myself next to the limo along with the rest of the agents, and we all watched while the president shook hands. I remember one of the women who was holding the sign remarked, "It worked, our sign worked." I noticed Dave Powers was standing in the rear of the follow-up car taking movies, which he did off and on throughout the entire motorcade.

Soon we were on the move again, going fast enough that I dropped back and returned to my position on the right rear running board of Halfback. I could tell we were getting closer to downtown Dallas, because the buildings were getting taller and the crowds were getting larger. I saw a multistoried glass skyscraper that stood out maybe two or more blocks away, directly to our right. I pointed it out to SA Ready, noting that there were even people standing on the rooftop.

We had now reached a point along the motorcade route where the crowds really started to thicken. In some instances, people had forced their way so far into the street that the motorcycle escorts beside the president's limo and Halfback could not get through, and they had to drop back behind our follow-up car. Each time this situation occurred, Clint would jump off of our vehicle and run up to take a position on the left rear step of the president's limo, placing himself closer to Mrs. Kennedy. *Something for my memory bank*, I thought, and continued concentrating on the crowd on my side of the road.

The motorcycles had maneuvered their way back into position and were starting to make a right turn. I took a quick glance at the street sign. MAIN STREET, it read. *Every city has a Main Street*, I thought, and I quickly turned my attention back to the crowd, which was now even bigger. As the motorcycles turned, the president's limo followed, and SA Sam Kinney kept the follow-up car glued to the limo's bumper, with no more than three to five feet separating the two vehicles. This is the way it had been throughout the entire motorcade, even at our higher speeds. There was no way Sam was going to let anything get between us and the president, no matter what speed we traveled. SA Kinney and SA Greer had spent hours practicing together, and they were a superior driving team.

After we completed the turn, I could hardly believe what I saw. Thousands of people packed the sidewalks on both sides, and the crowd spilled out into the street. Main Street was four lanes wide and was so packed with people that there was barely a lane wide enough for the president's limo to get through. People were on fire escapes and rooftops, hanging out of windows, you name it. There were even some people on top of a theater marquee. The sidewalks were solid. Anywhere there was a place to stand, someone was standing. They were all cheering at the top of their lungs, and clapping too. The growling of the motorcycle escort engines added to the pitched decibel level—all this fuss over the Kennedys. I could not imagine what it would be like if this were an unfriendly environment.

At one point, I remember an overeager teenage boy came out of the crowd. He had a camera in his hand and he was running toward the president's limo. SA Ready was closest in line of sight, so I pointed the boy out. SA Ready nodded, stepped off the running board, intercepted the boy, gave him a gentle nudge, and then jumped back onto the running board, barely missing a beat. "Well done," I said, while feeling kind of sorry for the kid, who had tumbled back into the crowd. I hoped he was OK, but he should have known better.

We had completed our pass through the heart of downtown Dallas and were now slowing down to make another turn, this time to the right onto Houston Street. The crowd had thinned considerably, but I was still concentrating on the people along my side of the follow-up car, watching for signs of anything harmful. We slowed down even more as we approached another turn, this one to the left. I got a quick glance out of the corner of my eye of an orangish-colored brick building that was going to be on my side of the road after we completed the turn, but I was too focused on what was immediately in front of me, so I didn't think twice about it. We slowed down even more and were barely moving at a snail's pace as SAs Greer and Kinney maneuvered the president's limo and our follow-up car around a sharp, almost complete hair-pin turn to the left. That's all I saw of the brick building before some trees along the sidewalk obscured my view. The only thing visible through the trees was the building's ground-floor facade, which appeared to be made of gray concrete blocks in some sort of crisscross pattern.

There were even fewer people along the sidewalk here, so at this point I started to scan ahead. We were approaching an open and sloping grassy area that was on my side of the road. I made a quick scan ahead toward the slope, and seeing nothing out of the ordinary, I continued scanning to my left toward the front of the cars. The lead car and the president's car had already straight-ened out from making their turn, and Halfback was just lining up behind them. The three vehicles were heading down a slight decline toward an underpass. SA Lawson radioed ahead to the Trade Mart to give them our five-minute arrival alert. We had two miles to go.

As a note to the reader, articulating all the thoughts, feelings, emotions, and actions that I witnessed during the next six sec-onds is difficult for me to express and keep in some semblance of order. Everything happened so fast.

BAM!

I heard the sound of a high-powered rifle being fired, coming from behind us, from over my right shoulder.

"What was that, a firecracker?" SA Ready asked. My mind was already racing, processing thoughts in milliseconds. Firecracker? Cherry bomb? M-80? I didn't see any smoke.

"I don't think so," I replied, already knowing in my mind that it wasn't a firecracker. It was a gunshot, and one coming from a high-powered rifle. I recognized it immediately from having grown up with guns and fired many. This was definitely the sound of a high-powered rifle. Ironically, only the day before, I had been talking with that Houston detective about hunting. Today was supposed to be the first day of deer season, so thoughts of a rifle shot immediately flashed through my mind.

When the first gunshot was fired, I was looking toward the front of the motorcade. I had just completed my scan from the building we had passed, scanning from right to left over the grassy area that I had seen only seconds earlier, and I was now scanning up over the top of an underpass that was directly ahead of us. I had just started to scan back to my right and my eyes were passing over the president's limo as the shot rang out. I immediately turned, looking over my right shoulder toward the direction of the sound.

I saw nothing. There were no obvious signs of a disturbance. Besides, we were moving, and there was no time to dwell on one particular area. I quickly looked at the limo and saw President Kennedy leaning to the left and raising his arms. I thought he was turning around to see where the noise came from. At the time, I did not realize that he had already been hit by a bullet.

I turned my head to look back toward the area where the sound had come from. I was searching for some sign of danger, a disturbance, a clue, anything that would help me find the source of the sound. All I saw were people running, scattering, and diving to the ground. I made another quick glance at the building that we had passed and still did not pick up on anything unusual. I was scanning fast. We were moving and I was trying to cover as much of the area as possible. I looked again back to my left, hoping to find something that I might have previously missed. I knew we were under attack by someone somewhere in the vicinity. The seconds were ticking away, and I couldn't spot anything.

My eyes returned to the front, and I saw Clint sprinting toward the president's limo. He was doing what every Secret Service agent was trained to do. He must have jumped from his position on Halfback's left front running board the split second after the first shot, because he was already in full stride, speeding toward SS-100-X, racing in his leather-soled dress shoes, suit, and tie. He was the only agent who had half a chance of reaching the limo. God forbid he should trip and fall. If that happened, I knew we would run over him. We couldn't stop and wouldn't stop no matter what.

Go, Clint, go, Clint, go, buddy, go, I was thinking, urging him on under my breath.

I knew that there was no way I could make it from where I stood on the right rear running board of Halfback. I had a bad angle, and we were moving too fast. SA Ready was in front of me. He had jumped off the running board, but ATSAIC Roberts had called him back for the same reason. There was no way he could make it either. I had this useless and helpless feeling. I was stuck in a position where I couldn't respond or do anything.

I was continuing my scan across the underpass that we were approaching. Clint was running, his arms outstretched, reaching for the leftmost grab bar on the trunk of SS-100-X.

The grab bars were there for Secret Service agents to hold on to while standing on the steps on the back of the limo whenever they weren't running or jogging along beside it during a motorcade such as ours. However, on November 22, 1963, there were no agents on the back of the limo, because President Kennedy did not want them there. The president did not want anyone blocking him from the public's view. This all came about at the president's request less than a week earlier during a motorcade in Tampa, Florida. All of us knew that it was an added security risk, but if that's what the president wanted, we all acceded. We really had no choice.

Just as Clint's fingertips touched the grab bar, he stumbled, but he managed to keep his balance and was able to grab hold of the bar and hang on at the same moment that SA Bill Greer hit the accelerator. At this point I thought that Lady Luck was on our side. I don't know if anyone other than the passengers inside the president's limo even realized that the president had already been hit. I certainly didn't. I just knew that we had to get out of there fast.

Clint was now starting to pull himself up onto the trunk of SS-100-X and we began to accelerate when—*BAM!*—a second shot rang out. The second shot also came from behind, but it sounded louder than the first one. It also had a different feeling, a different reverberation. It was still the sound of a high-powered rifle, but it was definitely different from the first. Maybe it was because of our location. We were now closer to the underpass and not in the open as much.

Agent Clint Hill jumps on the presidential limousine after John Kennedy is shot, Dallas, Texas, November 22, 1963. *AP Photo / James W. "Ike" Altgens*

All I was thinking was *faster, faster, faster* as I dismissed the thought of an echo from the first shot, because the time delay was too long. All these thoughts were flashing through my mind. We couldn't get out of the area fast enough.

I was looking forward and had a clear view of the president's limo in front of us. It was probably no more than fifty feet from my position on the right rear running board of Halfback to the back of the right rear seat in the president's limo. From where I was, I saw no disturbance in the limo. Everything still looked the same. President Kennedy was still seated fairly upright, leaning against Mrs. Kennedy with his head tilted slightly back. Mrs. Kennedy had her arm around his shoulders, and Clint was almost on top of the limo's trunk. I thought that the shot had missed.

In my mind I was still trying to dismiss the reality of what was actually happening, even though I knew better. I even tried to look at the tires on the limo, looking for signs of a blowout. I knew there wasn't one, but I looked anyway. I also had this strange sensation that is difficult for me to explain. As I recall these events, it's like I am removed from the scene yet still in it, like I am watching myself as everything unfolds in front of me. We had only traveled a short distance over a short period of time, but everything seemed like it was happening in slow motion, taking forever.

All thoughts of reaching safety vanished in the next moment, when Lady Luck skipped the scene. A third shot rang out, and the assassin's bullet found its mark. I saw a flash of white as the right side of President Kennedy's head exploded in a pink spray of blood, flesh, and brain matter. I automatically ducked, not wanting to get splattered as we drove through it. The president slumped to his left and out of sight. Clint had managed to pull himself up and was now on top of the trunk just as Mrs. Kennedy started to crawl out over the back, as if reaching for something.

Clint managed to push her back down into the rear seat and straddled the seat, covering her and the president with his body.

Everything that happened, from the first shot fired up to now, had only taken a matter of five or six seconds, and we were now zooming through an underpass at a high rate of speed. The last thing I remember seeing before passing through the underpass is one of our motorcycle escorts stopping by the curbside where the grassy area came down to meet the sidewalk and the street. A Black man dressed in green slacks and a tan shirt was running up the grassy slope toward a cement structure. There was a flash of darkness and roaring sounds, then daylight as we emerged on the other side of the underpass.

SA Ready and I were still standing on the running board when ATSAIC Roberts asked if anyone got the exact time of the shooting. I was wondering who in the hell had the presence of mind to check their watch under the circumstances when someone else replied 12:30 PM. Then someone told me to get inside the car, and SA Bennett pulled me by the arm. My sunglasses fell off in the process, and SA Bennett quickly picked them up and handed them back. Then I held on to SA Ready's arm as he climbed over the door and into the backseat. This is a small detail, but it illustrates how clear some of the events of that fateful day remain in my mind, even today, nearly sixty years later.

We were now speeding along on an expressway, and I noticed a small family-sized group standing by an intersection waving to us. As we flew by, I remember thinking, *Poor them, they have no idea what has just happened, or where we are headed, or why we are driving by so quickly.* I had no idea where we were going either. We were no longer on the designated motorcade route. I only assumed that we were headed to the nearest hospital. Not that we needed to rush. I saw the third shot hit President Kennedy in the head, and I saw the results of the wound. There was no way that President Kennedy could survive a hit like that and still be alive. No way! The massive head wound that he had received just blew his head wide open. Clint confirmed my thoughts when he looked back toward Halfback, lying on top of the trunk, and shook his head from side to side, giving us a thumbs-down signal.

I had drawn my revolver at some point after being pulled back into Halfback, but I don't remember doing it. I saw that SA Bennett had his revolver out too. I realized that it was both ridiculous and useless, so I re-holstered mine.

We were now traveling at a high rate of speed, and I turned to look back to the rear. I wanted to see what was happening behind us, because Vice President Johnson and Lady Bird had been in the car following Halfback throughout the motorcade. They were still behind us, but we had put quite a distance between the two cars.

ATSAIC Roberts started giving general instructions to his detail agents to cover Vice President Johnson as soon as we stopped. We started to slow down, and I turned back to look to the front to see what was happening. The brake lights on the president's limo were on, and we were slowing down to make a right-hand turn. After making the turn, we headed toward some buildings, which I assumed belonged to the closest hospital.

11

PARKLAND

THE PRESIDENTIAL LIMO and Secret Service follow-up car came
to an abrupt stop. It was 12:38 PM central standard time. The
forward momentum of the stop was so great that it knocked me
off balance. I was glad that I had been holding on to the grab bar
in front of me; otherwise, I might have ended up in the front seat.

We were at the emergency entrance to Parkland Memorial Hospital. The two cars had come to a stop, one behind the other, next
to a covered walkway leading into the entryway. The walkway was
already lined with people, some dressed in medical garb and others dressed in civilian clothes. It had only been five minutes or so
since leaving Dealey Plaza and already people were waiting for us.

Until a few moments ago I had been living my dream, but
now my dream had turned into a living nightmare.

The two cars had barely stopped when SA Ready opened the
right rear door of the follow-up car and was out in a flash. He
went to his left, to where ASAIC Roy Kellerman and ATSAIC
Emory Roberts had both disembarked and were talking. I immediately jumped out behind him. If I headed to my left toward the
president's car, I knew I would be caught in a jam of people, so
I decided that it would be faster to turn right and go around the
rear of the follow-up car to get to the First Lady.

I heard ATSAIC Roberts and ASAIC Kellerman discussing assignments. It was imperative now to protect Vice President Johnson, even though he had his own security team. Roberts was sending SA Ready and the rest of his shift to cover Vice President and Mrs. Johnson. I knew these instructions did not include me. My place was with the First Lady. Without hesitation, I continued to run around the rear of the follow-up car and raced to the president's limo. Clint had already slid off the trunk of SS-100-X and had gone around to the right side of the limo to assist with the removal of President Kennedy's body.

When I reached the car, Mrs. Kennedy was seated sideways with her back toward me and the left rear door. She was holding what was left of the president's head in her lap, bending over trying to cover it. I reached over the side of the closed door, took her gently by the shoulders in an attempt to help her up. I said, "Come on, Mrs. Kennedy, let me help you."

She wouldn't budge. I couldn't see her face, but I heard her say firmly, "No, I want to stay with him." I let go.

Realizing that I needed to do something different to get the First Lady to safety, I grabbed the door handle and yanked the door open. Just then, Clint arrived and took over. He had come around from behind me and stepped inside the large backseat area ahead of me, past Mrs. Kennedy, closer to the president's body. The situation was fluid—others were trying to remove the body.

I stepped into the limo behind Clint. I was scanning everything in sight. The first thing I noticed was a small splintered crack in the front windshield. It was located to the left of the rearview mirror on the driver's side. I immediately assumed that it had been made by a ricocheting bullet fragment. *How on earth could a bullet fragment have flown up there without hitting someone?* I wondered.

Looking up, I saw SA Win Lawson. He was running along the walkway coming toward us, pushing a gurney. He was followed by another person dressed in hospital garb who was also pushing a gurney. *Two gurneys, why two gurneys?*

My thoughts were cut short. I looked at Governor Connally. Seated directly in front of the president, he was slumped to the side. He must have turned at some point. His white shirt had bright red bloodstains. Good God, had he had been hit too, or was he just splattered with the president's blood? I then realized that he had also been shot, probably by the second bullet, and his body was blocking the right rear door of the limo.

SA Lawson arrived with his gurney, and other agents quickly started to move Governor Connally onto it. Once that task was completed, Mrs. Connally stood up and exited the limo, following the governor's gurney as they raced toward the emergency entrance. With Governor Connally out of the way, the pathway was clear enough for agents to get to the president.

While all of this was happening, Mrs. Kennedy continued to cradle her husband's head. The president's body wasn't going anywhere until Mrs. Kennedy released him. Clint kept urging her to let go, while I scanned the inside of the car and the surrounding outside area.

The entire scene was crazy and awful. Pieces of pink flesh, gray brain matter, and blood were splattered everywhere. They clung to the backseats and all over the right rear door panel. It was a mess, an ugly, bloody mess. Continuing my surveillance, I looked back toward the follow-up car. It was now empty, and there were no agents in sight.

I returned my attention to the presidential limo. Looking down at the seat beside Mrs. Kennedy, I saw two brass bullet fragments sitting in a pool of bright red blood. I could hardly believe it. They glistened like two gold nuggets in their blood-red surroundings. I bent over, picked up the largest of the two pieces, and examined it. It was about the size of the end of my little finger. It looked like a small mushroom that had been squashed. I quickly replaced it exactly where I had found it.

About then, even though only seconds had passed, Clint finally convinced Mrs. Kennedy to let go of the president's head. When she released it, someone said, "Cover up his head." Thinking quickly and without hesitating, Clint removed his suit coat and covered the president's head and upper torso. None of us wanted anyone to see the president in this condition. Then Clint, ASAIC Kellerman, and SA Lawson were finally able to remove the president's lifeless body from the backseat area of the limo and place it onto a gurney.

Dave Powers, the president's special assistant and longtime friend, was leaning over the president as they removed his body and kept repeating over and over, "Oh no! Mr. President! Mr. President, oh no!"

When Mrs. Kennedy finally stood up, I looked again at the seat and saw a bullet on top of the tufted black leather cushioning behind where she had been sitting. It was resting in a seam where the tufted leather padding ended against the car's metal body. It wasn't a bullet fragment like the other two pieces. It was a completely intact bullet. It had been hidden behind Mrs. Kennedy all the time she was seated. No wonder I hadn't seen it sooner.

I picked it up and quickly examined it. It was approximately two inches long and in almost perfect condition. It was not distorted in any way and had rifle striations running lengthwise along the sides. *Man, oh man, oh man*, I thought. *What should I do?*

Seconds were ticking away, things were moving fast, and I had to make a quick decision. All sorts of thoughts and what-ifs were running through my mind. Three shots . . . bullet fragments . . . and now a completely intact bullet. This was IMPORTANT EVIDENCE. My mind was spinning, processing thoughts and information, while I continued to scan the area looking for other special agents.

Exhibit 399, the bullet Special Agent Paul Landis found in the limousine, Dallas, Texas, November 22, 1963. *National Archives, Ce399-1, courtesy of Wikimedia Commons*

The vice president's limo had yet to arrive, so there were no agents from his detail in sight. In fact, there were no other agents in sight anywhere to the rear, to my right, or to the front. *Where are they? Where the hell is SA Greer? He was driving the president's limo. He should be here.* The follow-up car was empty too. *Where the hell is Special Agent Sam Kinney? He was driving it. Jeez, oh man! Where the hell is everyone? Where did all the agents go? Who is going to secure the car AND THE CRIME SCENE?* Everyone seemed to be crowded around the president's body. No one was paying attention to anything else.

My immediate concern was the bullet. It would be visible to anyone happening to walk by. *What about photographers? Or worse yet, What about a souvenir hunter?* Thoughts continued to race through my mind.

People were starting to mill around and beginning to merge toward the car. I had to do something, and I had to do it fast. I was afraid this nearly perfectly intact bullet would disappear. I did not want that to happen. Clint was occupied helping Mrs. Kennedy out of the limo. She was already halfway out of the car, and I had to stay with Clint and her. *Damn it, damn it, Paul, decision time.*

All this time I had been holding the bullet in my hand, but instead of reaching down and replacing the bullet where I had found it, like I had done with the bullet fragment, I slipped it into my right suit coat pocket. All of this had taken place in a fraction of seconds. I would give the bullet to ASAIC Kellerman, I thought, and explain my actions later, when there was time.

Everything was happening quickly, and as I rushed to keep up with Clint and Mrs. Kennedy, I noticed Mrs. Kennedy had left her clutch purse and her pink Oleg Cassini pillbox hat on the back-seat. Obviously, these items were the last thing on her mind, so I picked up both of them to take with us. There was also a Zippo cigarette lighter lying on the seat. It had a shiny chrome finish that was now stained with the president's blood. It was resting against the backseat cushion, so I picked it up too. I turned it over in my hand and saw the presidential seal on the opposite side. Knowing that Mrs. Kennedy had an occasional smoke, I assumed that the lighter had slipped out of her purse. *Well, Mrs. Kennedy doesn't need to see this reminder*, I thought, and I slipped the lighter into the same pocket that held the bullet. I would give the lighter to Provi, her personal assistant, once we returned to the White House. (Author's note: It was almost fifty years later when I learned from Clint that the Zippo was actually *his* lighter and that it must have slipped out of his suit jacket when he covered the president's head. *Duh*, I thought. *I should have known.* He also told me that Provi had since sold the lighter on eBay.)

The bouquet of roses that had been presented to Mrs. Kennedy upon her arrival at Love Field also lay in disarray on the backseat. *They can stay*, I thought. Today, black-and-white photos of the flowers exist that were taken at the time, but they are staged photos. In them the bouquet is intact. That wasn't the case when I last saw them as we were leaving the limo. The bouquet was scattered when we arrived at Parkland.

Stepping out of the limo with purse and hat in hand, the bullet and lighter secure in my suit coat pocket, I followed Mrs. Kennedy. I moved to her left side, and everyone headed toward the emergency room entrance. Mrs. Kennedy was now on my right, next to the gurney that was carrying the lifeless body of her husband. Only minutes had passed since the shooting.

The cortege of people consisting of Secret Service agents, hospital staff, and I don't know who else burst through the emergency entrance doors like a runaway train. I mean, we were really flying. The entrance lobby was utter confusion, created mostly by the way we blasted through the entrance, and probably by Governor Connally's entrance prior to ours. People were scattering everywhere to get out of our way, most of them hospital staff who were rushing in to see what all the commotion was about.

I think it was sometime immediately after our entrance that I handed Mrs. Kennedy her purse and hat, but I don't recall exactly because of all the chaos and confusion. It was really hectic, and I was running and yelling, "Out of the way! Get out of the way!" I spotted a group of gawkers who were ahead of us, standing in what appeared to be a hallway entrance. A nurse was now running along beside me, and I grabbed a corner of her uniform sleeve to get her attention and asked her to please disperse the small group and help us clear the area. A flurry of blue, green, and white faceless hospital uniforms moved. A pathway cleared and we were able to get through.

I had no idea where we were headed, but by God, I did know that the way we were moving, nothing was going to get in our way to stop us. I just followed the gurney and made sure I stayed close to Mrs. Kennedy. We angled to the right as we crossed through the entrance lobby and headed down a short corridor to a doorway on the left with the number 1 on it. The doorway was on the left side of the corridor, so in order to pass through, the gurney had to be pivoted ninety degrees. Even then, it was a tight fit, with no room to spare along the sides for people to get through. Once the gurney was turned, everyone in our initial group, plus those extras who had joined us, tried to jam their way through the doorway all at once. Mrs. Kennedy had to drop back behind the gurney in order to enter the room, and I stepped up behind her to prevent her from being jostled by the now rude and unruly collection of people.

Once she was inside the room, Mrs. Kennedy stepped to her left and stood beside the entrance door while people continued to push and shove their way past her. As I entered—or, more to the point, was pushed into—the trauma room, the president's lifeless body was already being lifted off the gurney and placed onto a white cotton blanket that covered the surface of a stainless-steel examination table in the middle of the room. All sorts of medical apparatuses were at the end of the table where they had placed the president's head. The gurney which had carried the president's body into the room was then pushed aside and up against a beige tiled wall by the doorway inside the room, partially blocking the doorway. I'm guessing the trauma room was maybe twenty by twenty feet square.

The gurney, located where it was, took up precious space inside the room; it also made it more difficult for people to enter or exit. Only no one was exiting! People continued pushing, shoving, and shouting, trying to get into a space that was already cramped.

What is wrong with all these people? I wondered. *Have they no respect?*

By now, I had been pushed up against the examination table and was tightly wedged against it, trapped right next to the president's feet. I turned my head to check on Mrs. Kennedy. She was still standing safely beside the doorway, having avoided all the pushing and shoving, but her face was expressionless. She appeared to be removed, unaware of the chaos happening in front of her. At least she wasn't trapped and being jostled by the rude crowd; I was relieved to see that she was safe in that respect. I glanced around looking for Clint but did not see him.

We were all packed together in the room, shoulder to shoulder, like sardines in a can. Everyone's attention was focused on the president's head, which doctors were already examining. It seemed like everyone in the room was craning their necks trying to see the president's head wound. Not me; I had seen enough outside when we were in the limo. I knew that if I looked now, I would probably pass out. Even the thought of it made me feel faint. I had to look down and away. I didn't dare pass out. What kind of person or agent would I be if I allowed that to happen? I had to hang in there, no matter what. I was feeling claustrophobic. Where the hell was Clint, anyway?

In order to keep from passing out or fainting, I focused in on the president's shoes. His feet were right by my side as he lay on the examination table. His shoes were black, and I wondered what brand, style, and size he wore. From the way the president's body had been placed, his left pant leg was pulled up above his black socks, and I even thought of reaching over to pull the pant leg down to cover the skin that was showing. All these mundane thoughts were going through my mind while people continued to push and shove.

Just then another person was trying to push his way into the room, loudly announcing, "I am a doctor. I am a doctor. Please, please let me through. I need to get through." More pushing and shoving ensued as people tried to make room, but there was no place to go. *Jesus, what is wrong with these people?* Then the doctor who was already at the head of the examination table called out, "PLEASE, PLEASE, EVERYONE, PLEASE, WE NEED ROOM TO WORK!"

Everything was happening so rapidly that there was hardly time to think. Only seconds had passed, and I was fumbling with the bullet in my pocket while I was concentrating on the president's shoes. For whatever reason, my thoughts shifted. *This is where the bullet belongs, with the president's body. This bullet is important evidence. A doctor will find it, and it might be helpful during the autopsy.*

People were starting to leave the room. I had to make another split-second decision. *Just do it, Paul. Just do it. If you are going to do anything, you've got to do it now, before the opportunity slips away.*

I removed the bullet from my pocket, and reaching out over the examination table, I carefully placed it on the white cotton blanket next to the president's left shoe. When I let go, the bullet started rolling toward the edge of the table. *Holy shit*, I thought, as my heart jumped and started racing. I quickly reached back and stopped it from rolling just before it fell into a little trough that ran around the edge of the table. If it had fallen into that trough, or, worse yet, onto the floor, I knew that I would not have had the time or ability to retrieve it.

When the president's body had been placed on the examination table, it had made a small wrinkle in the cotton blanket by the president's feet. Because of this, I was able to reposition the bullet to prevent it from rolling again. With all the confusion going on in the room, no one had even noticed what I had done.

Whew, that was close, I thought. The last thing I wanted was for that bullet to get lost.

I felt relief. I was certain at the time that I had made the correct decision. I had saved an important piece of evidence, and I had placed it where it belonged, with the president's body. It would be found and prove to be helpful. I felt like a heavy burden had been lifted from my shoulders.

I turned, looking for Mrs. Kennedy. All those people who previously couldn't wait to enter Trauma Room #1 were now pushing and shoving trying to make a hasty exit. Only now, the empty gurney by the entrance was making exiting more difficult. I was finally able to move, and I stepped to the side and stood between Mrs. Kennedy and the doorway until most of the people left the room.

When Mrs. Kennedy was ready to leave, I was at her side. Our time in Trauma Room #1 had been brief, probably no more than a minute, but for me it felt like an eternity.

As we were leaving the trauma room, Mrs. Kennedy stopped and hesitated in the doorway. I continued around and past her and was asking someone to find a chair for her when, at the same time, someone else was already arriving with a chair. Clearly other people had the same thought.

Mrs. Kennedy came out and the door closed. Now weary looking, she sat down on the chair that had been provided. Several people were still milling around the area, and with the help of a nurse, I was able to clear most of them away.

I finally spotted Clint. He had been running along beside the right side of the gurney while we raced through the emergency room lobby, but I had lost track of him when we entered the trauma room. I'm guessing that he had either been blocked out by the crowd or left the trauma room before I had a chance to see him. Either way, he and ASAIC Kellerman were talking to each other in a hallway located to my left. Clint was wearing a suit coat jacket. It never dawned on me that his own jacket was still in Trauma Room #1, covered in blood. Where had this one come from?

I headed over to talk to them when the trauma door flew open and someone rushed out asking if anyone knew the president's blood type. Kellerman and Clint simultaneously reached for their wallets, but Kellerman beat Clint to the draw and came up with the information first. "O. Rh positive" was his reply. That was something I never knew, and realized I'd better learn Mrs. Kennedy's blood type, just in case.

Clint was busy doing everything possible to assist ASAIC Kellerman. The two of them had access to a vacant doctor's office near the trauma room. The office had a telephone, and they already had an open line connected directly to the White House switchboard. Clint moved into the office, and I followed him. I only had a brief moment to tell him where I would be before returning to Mrs. Kennedy's side.

Then a different person came out of Trauma Room #1 and said that the president was still breathing. Mrs. Kennedy stood up and asked, "Do you mean he still may be alive?" but she sat down again when no one answered.

I was already resigned to the fact that the president had probably died the instant the third shot hit him in the head. If it had been anyone other than the president's life on the line, they probably would have declared him dead on arrival when we first got to the hospital.

Then Vice President Johnson was whisked by, bent over and shielded by several detail agents. They were really moving, and I had no idea where they were taking him. They all disappeared down the same hallway where Kellerman and Clint had been standing.

I returned my focus to Mrs. Kennedy. Several people were still hanging around, so I commandeered a doctor to help clear the area. After that, I grabbed an empty chair and took a two o'clock position about ten or fifteen feet in front of Mrs. Kennedy. This gave her some private space, plus my position also provided a better observation point for the emergency room and the surroundings.

Glancing at Mrs. Kennedy, I thought she looked quite regal, sitting on her chair, back straight and hands folded in her lap, but her face was expressionless. There were no tears in her eyes, just a blank and distant look, like she wasn't even there. What thoughts had to be going through her mind, I wondered.

I knew nothing about shock or how to recognize its symptoms, but if I were to guess, I would say that Mrs. Kennedy had to be in shock.

At the time, I was not concerned about any outside harm coming to Mrs. Kennedy. I knew that she was relatively safe where we were inside Parkland Memorial Hospital. I just wanted to keep people from crowding around and bothering her and allow her some space. My main concern was me. I was fighting my own battle. I couldn't get the head shot that I had witnessed out of my mind. It kept repeating itself over and over like a looping newsreel clip. I struggled to keep from falling apart and passing out. Several times I nearly broke down.

Come on, Paul, I kept urging myself. *Be strong. Hang in there. Don't break down now. Don't be an embarrassment. Think about Mrs. Kennedy and her safety. You have a job to do.* Somehow, all these thoughts managed to help me hang in there.

Mrs. Kennedy reentered the trauma room a couple of times, but only for a brief moment each time. At one point, she stood up and walked across the emergency room to a curtained area and stood by a table staring at the wall. I approached her and asked if there was anything I could do. She just shook her head no, so I retreated, leaving her to her thoughts. Vice President Johnson's wife, Lady Bird, appeared at one point and talked to Mrs. Kennedy while she was sitting by the trauma room door.

It was confusing and there was a lot going on, and a lot of the details I just don't remember. I don't recall the priests arriving to administer the last rites; however, I do remember the big discussion that followed. I had returned to the hallway, and everyone was expressing a different opinion as to what time to declare as the "official time of death." There were logistics that had to be considered, both political and religious. The time of the priests' arrival, the reading of the last rites, what to tell the press, what to tell the public—all sorts of details had to be put into proper sequence. It had to appear that there had been a valid attempt to save the president, but without success. The official time of death was finally agreed upon—1:00 PM central standard time. If they had asked me, I would have replied, "12:30 PM, in Dealey Plaza."

Also, at that time, no one knew who was behind the assassination, and it was decided that the best thing to do was to get Vice President Johnson back to Washington and the White House as soon as possible. That was fine with the vice president, but he was determined to have Mrs. Kennedy return to Washington with him. However, Mrs. Kennedy was equally as determined not to return to Washington or even leave the hospital without her husband's body. The Dallas County medical examiner, who had arrived on the scene earlier, intervened, telling everyone that they were not allowed to leave the hospital with the president's body until an autopsy had been performed. At the time this was a state law in Texas. There had been no autopsy performed, only a desperate attempt to save the president's life.

According to Clint, in his book *Mrs. Kennedy and Me*, at some point after we arrived at Parkland, Ken O'Donnell, the president's friend and chief adviser, had instructed him to order a casket.

Clint called a local establishment—O'Neal's Funeral Home. Subsequently, an all-bronze casket was delivered and taken directly into Trauma Room #1.

So while the president's body was being prepared for removal, an argument ensued in the hallway outside of the trauma room entrance. Texas authorities wanted the president's body to remain in Texas. He was the victim of a homicide, and there had to be an autopsy. White House staff and Secret Service personnel were equally insistent in their argument: This was the body of a president of the United States, and thus an exception to the Texas rule. The autopsy would be performed in Washington at Bethesda Naval Hospital.

Clint and I stood by listening as the discussion became heated. Tempers were starting to flare, and I thought that a major altercation was going to escalate into something worse. The trauma room door opened, and a casket on top of a gurney appeared in the doorway. Secret Service agents who were in the area immediately stepped to its side and took command.

I don't remember any concessions being made or how the argument was finally settled, or if it actually was. All I remember is that Mrs. Kennedy had rejoined the group, and I followed Clint and the casket alongside Mrs. Kennedy as we headed down the hallway to an emergency room exit, different from the one we had used when we first arrived. Texas state law be damned, the president's body was returning to Washington with us.

The white Cadillac hearse that had earlier delivered the empty casket from O'Neal's Funeral Home was outside and waiting, and the same casket, now containing the body of the president, was placed inside the rear compartment. The president's physician, Admiral George Burkley, who accompanied the president on all his trips, Mrs. Kennedy, and Clint wedged themselves into the rear compartment with the casket. ATSAIC Stout and ASAIC

Kellerman climbed into the front seat beside SA Andy Berger, who was sitting behind the steering wheel. I jumped into an official car being driven by SA Greer. We were directly behind the ambulance, and at 2:04 PM central standard time, we departed Parkland Memorial Hospital for the ten-minute ride to Love Field.

About a half an hour earlier, at 1:35 PM, agents had whisked Vice President and Mrs. Johnson away from Parkland Memorial Hospital in two unmarked cars. They took them to Love Field, where they waited on board AF 26000 for Mrs. Kennedy's arrival. When we arrived, SA Berger parked the hearse near the boarding ramp located at the rear of the plane. While agents carried the heavy bronze casket up the ramp, I stood at the bottom with Mrs. Kennedy, and the two of us watched as the agents struggled, trying to fit the casket through the airplane door. Once the casket was finally on board, Mrs. Kennedy climbed the steps and I followed.

Mrs. Kennedy boarding Air Force One at Love Field, Dallas, Texas, November 22, 1963. *Photo by Cecil W. Stoughton, John F. Kennedy Presidential Library, courtesy of Wikimedia Commons*

When I reached the top, I headed directly to the passenger area located in the front section of the aircraft. ASAIC Kellerman was standing in the first row of seats on the right. His back was against the bulkhead that separated the cockpit and steward's area from the rest of the plane. An air force steward was in the aisle behind him, filling empty glasses with ice at a service station. Kellerman beckoned me to come forward. I slid into the second row of seats facing him and collapsed in the seat next to the window. As soon as my rear end hit the cushion, I turned my face toward the window and began to cry.

At first, I was embarrassed, breaking down in front of everyone, but I couldn't help it. The sobs came and the tears flowed. *Some tough guy you are*, I thought, but I didn't care. I had come so close to breaking down earlier that I was just thankful that I had been able to hold my emotions together until now. I stared out the window, lost in thoughts about Mrs. Kennedy and her now fatherless children, Caroline and John Jr., and I wondered what the future held for them. All the time, visions of President Kennedy's head exploding replayed over and over, again and again. I just couldn't shake them.

I became aware of someone in the seat next to me and turned to see SA Bennett. *How ironic*, I thought. *Here we are, seated side by side, just like on our way to the hospital.* Only this time, he wasn't holding his Colt .38 Special, he was holding a pen. He was writing notes regarding the events of the past few hours into his pocket-sized memorandum book, the one each of us carried to keep track of our daily activities. *He's doing what I should be doing. He's doing what any good agent should be doing.* I turned away and continued to look out the window for the next half hour, completely oblivious to what else was happening elsewhere on the plane. *I can write my notes later.*

I was aware that we were still sitting on the ground, but I was not aware of the reason. We were waiting for a federal judge to arrive and swear in Vice President Johnson as our next president. When the judge arrived, I was still looking out the airplane window, deep in my own sorrow and thoughts.

ASAIC Kellerman gently shook me by the shoulder to get my attention. He said, "C'mon, Paul, you've got to witness this. Vice President Johnson is going to be sworn in as president. This is history in the making."

I couldn't have cared less. I'd already witnessed enough first-hand history that day. I continued staring out the window. Kellerman persisted, and I eventually got out of my seat, and we

Lyndon Baines Johnson is sworn in as president aboard Air Force One, Dallas, Texas, November 22, 1963. Special Agent Paul Landis observed the event from the doorway at the back. *Photo by Cecil W. Stoughton, LBJ Presidential Library, courtesy of Wikimedia Commons*

walked toward the rear of the plane to the bulkhead. SA Lem Johns and ASAIC Kellerman filled the bulkhead doorway in front of me, forcing me to peek around them to witness the event. At 2:38 PM, in a solemn ceremony, federal judge Sarah T. Hughes administered the presidential oath of office to Lyndon B. Johnson, making him the thirty-sixth president of the United States.

Judge Hughes left the plane, and I returned to my window seat and began to cry again. At 2:47 PM, we were airborne.

I vaguely remember ASAIC Kellerman bringing me a prepared scotch and soda. Whether he spoke to me or tried to encourage me in some other way to come out of my funk, I don't remember. I took the drink, so I must have drunk it, but I simply don't remember anything else about the flight back to Washington, DC.

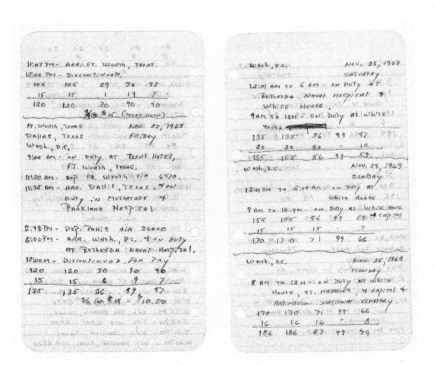

Completed memo notes after return to DC. *Author's collection*

12

BACK IN WASHINGTON, DC

A CHANGE IN MOTION and the sounds of Air Force One's landing gear engaging brought me back to the present and out of my funk, at least for the time being. We were preparing to land at Andrews Air Force Base. It was time for me to buckle up—and to buckle down.

We landed at 5:58 PM eastern standard time. As soon as Air Force One stopped rolling, I got out of my seat and headed back toward the bulkhead and the rear of the plane along with the rest of the agents and White House staff who were on board. The rear door of the plane was already open, and a hydraulic lift with a large boxlike container was easing up to the rear entrance.

I grabbed one of the handles on the side of the president's casket and was helping to lift it when the handle I was holding broke off. I looked down at the broken handle in my hand in utter disbelief. My immediate thought was *What a cheap and crummy casket to use for the president's return home*. However, I would later learn that the earlier struggle to get the casket on board Air Force One was because the handles made the casket too wide to fit through the narrow doorway of the plane. Agents had broken the handles off in Dallas in order to get the casket through the door. The handle in my hand must have been one that was cracked but never came off.

I turned and gave the handle to ASAIC Kellerman. He was right beside me and slipped the broken handle into his topcoat pocket while we, along with Mrs. Kennedy and several other people—including the president's brother, Robert Kennedy, who had come on board when we first landed—rode the lift to the ground.

A US Navy ambulance was waiting, and the casket was loaded into the rear. Mrs. Kennedy and her brother-in-law climbed in to be with the president's body. SA Bill Greer was already behind the steering wheel of the ambulance, and Kellerman signaled for me to slide into the front seat beside him. Admiral Burkley followed me, and then Kellerman climbed in too. At 6:10 PM, with the four of us squeezed together in the front seat of the ambulance and with Mrs. Kennedy, Robert Kennedy, and the president's body riding in the rear, we departed Andrews Air Force Base. We had a silent police escort, with only flashing lights. No one in the front seat of the ambulance had much to say as we rode in somber silence on our way to Bethesda Naval Hospital, where an autopsy would be performed.

For forty-five minutes I sat on the front edge of the ambulance seat with my body wedged against the dashboard, until we arrived at Bethesda at 6:55 PM. Clint and I escorted Mrs. Kennedy and Robert Kennedy up to the seventeenth floor of the hospital, where there was a presidential suite. We immediately secured the area, and from that point on, only hospital personnel assigned to the area, Kennedy family members, close friends, and authorized personnel were allowed.

I remained on the seventeenth floor for the next nine hours, leaving only twice. The first time I left was to locate ASAIC Kellerman in the hospital morgue and deliver a telephone message from Chief James Rowley. The second time I left was to locate a White House driver for our departure.

In the wee hours of the morning of November 23, 1963, a new casket bearing the body of President John F. Kennedy was again loaded into the rear of a US Navy ambulance. Mrs. Kennedy and her brother-in-law, Robert Kennedy, again climbed into the rear of an ambulance to be with the president's body. SA Bill Greer again slid into the driver's seat. It would be the last time he chauffeured the president and Mrs. Kennedy. Kellerman again took the right front passenger seat. Special Agent Clint Hill entered the first limousine behind the ambulance, and I entered the second.

Our small motorcade, with police escort, departed at 3:56 AM in somber silence. We arrived at the White House at 4:24 AM, where we were greeted by a US Marine Corps honor guard. The casket was removed from the ambulance, carried into the White House, and placed in the center of the East Room, where it remained for the next thirty-two hours.

Looking back at the events of sixty years ago, I don't know how I got through the days following the assassination, up to and including the funeral. When I got home to my apartment in Kensington, Maryland, that Saturday morning, November 23, I was emotionally drained and exhausted. But there was no time for sleep, and tired as I was, I doubt if I could have. I had four hours before I had to return to the White House. That was just enough time to grab something to eat, shower, shave, brush my teeth, and change clothes before returning to work. I remember my roommate SA Dick Johnsen being there, but I don't remember talking to him. He had worked the 4:00 PM–midnight shift at the White House and was asleep for most of the four hours I was home. My other roommate, SA Dave Grant, was still in Dallas assisting the Dallas Police Department with its investigation.

All three of us had been in Dallas on separate assignments. Dick had been at the Dallas Trade Mart with his regular shift and was also at Parkland Memorial Hospital; Dave had been on the advance team for the Dallas Trade Mart, and he too had been at Parkland; and I of course was with Mrs. Kennedy. I did not remember seeing either one of them the whole time the three of us were in Dallas.

The rest of that Saturday, I was at the White House. By the time I arrived at 9:00 AM, the transition of power was already in progress. President and Mrs. Johnson had not yet moved in, but the Oval Office was already being prepared for the new president. Many of John F. Kennedy's personal items had already been removed and taken to Clint's office, which was located in the Map Room near the South Portico entrance to the White House.

The mood among most agents in the White House that first Saturday morning after the assassination was anger. We were resentful of Johnson. We all knew that there was no love lost between him and the Kennedys. The angrier agents among us commented rashly that they wouldn't be surprised if Johnson had something to do with the events in Dallas. We all knew how badly he wanted to be president. But no one was serious, we were all just shocked, and saddened, and angry. There was no escaping the fact that the changeover was happening. Johnson was now the president.

That Saturday morning, I was informed that all agents who had been in Dallas were required to submit a brief summary report of their activities for Friday, November 22. While I was writing my report, I was also told that the Secret Service had obtained a film of the assassination taken by an amateur photographer who happened to be on the scene in Dealey Plaza. This is the now famous Zapruder film. All agents were required to view the film and sign off that they had seen it. It was mandatory. I didn't want to see it, and there was no way they were going to make me watch it. No follow-up ensued, and no one ever asked me about it. I eventually saw the film for the first time in 1972 when it was shown on television.

Sometime later that Saturday afternoon, Clint informed me that we were going to escort Mrs. Kennedy, Bobby Kennedy, and the late president's sisters Jean Smith and Pat Lawford to Arlington National Cemetery to select a grave site. Clint called for Mrs. Kennedy's limo and driver. He accompanied the family in the limousine, and I followed them in a Secret Service sedan that we usually used to transport Mrs. Kennedy or the children. I have no other memories of that event or of that day. My day finished around 10 PM, and I went home.

Early the next morning, Sunday, November 24, my roommate Dave finally got back from Dallas while I was getting ready to leave for work. When we saw each other, the two of us immediately started crying. We both sat down at the breakfast table and cried together, asking ourselves over and over, why, why, why? We didn't talk about the assassination or of the events that followed. Dave didn't talk about what he had done in Dallas, and I didn't talk about anything either. We just sat and cried.

When I returned to the White House and entered our Secret Service office off the West Wing lobby later that morning, the agents there were passing around a photograph of suspected assassin Lee Harvey Oswald. The photo showed the suspect standing by a wooden fence holding a rifle. Dave had brought the photograph back from Dallas earlier that day.

I grew up with guns. My father was a hunter and outdoorsman. He bought me my first BB gun before I was seven years old. It was a single-shot Daisy; later I got my real Red Ryder. When I turned nine, I went squirrel hunting and pheasant hunting with my dad for the first time. I had been interested in guns and hunting ever since, and by 1963 I had a small collection of my own guns in my Maryland apartment.

The rifle in the Oswald photograph looked familiar. I owned one just like it. It was a WWII surplus Italian Mannlicher-Carcano rifle. I had purchased mine in March 1958 from Golden State Arms Corp. in Pasadena, California, with an ad coupon from *American Rifleman* magazine. It was cheap, $12.95, plus for an additional $3.40, I got fifty-four rounds of military ammo and a free European bayonet. All this for only $16.35. The only difference was, mine was 7.35×51mm caliber and Oswald's was 6.5×52mm caliber. No one in the office had heard of this rifle, so I offered to bring mine in the following morning for examination. I can only imagine what would happen today if someone tried walking into the White House with a rifle like I did back in 1963, Secret Service agent or not.

That Sunday, preparations were also being made for the funeral procession that would take President Kennedy's body from the White House to lie in state in the Capitol Building's Rotunda. I was standing outside with SA Foster, SA Wells, and SA Meredith in front of the North Portico when someone came out of the White House shouting "Oswald's been shot." I knew there was a small black-and-white TV set in the head usher's office that was tuned to a live network broadcast originating from Dallas; I had seen it earlier on my way to join the others who were waiting outside. Now I ran up the steps of the North Portico and into the usher's office and watched a rerun of Oswald being shot.

I went back outside and shared what I had seen, and the four of us continued to wait. I was secretly glad that someone had shot the creep. If I'd had the chance, I probably would have done the same, not even thinking of the consequences or how it would have affected the investigation.

Eventually, an honor guard carried the casket out of the White House and placed it on a horse-drawn caisson, and at 1:08 PM the funeral procession began. We departed the White House grounds to the sounds of a slow drumbeat and the clip-clop of the horses' hooves landing on the pavement. Black Jack, the riderless horse with empty saddle and empty boots in the stirrups pointing backward to signify a fallen leader, pranced nervously behind the caisson. As we slowly headed toward the Capitol, thousands of people lined the sidewalks on both sides of Pennsylvania Avenue. The sound of silence hung heavily in the air as people crossed themselves, hugged each other, and cried when we passed by. I was riding in the front seat of a limo with Peter Lawford, President Kennedy's brother-in-law, seated in the rear. I have faint recollections of reaching the Capitol Building and joining Clint beside Mrs. Kennedy and of walking up the steps into the Rotunda, but I do not recall anything about being inside.

Special Agent Paul Landis (far left) speaks with Attorney General Robert F. Kennedy at the Capitol Building, November 24, 1963.
Photo by Abbie Rowe, Harry S. Truman Library, courtesy of Wikimedia Commons

After the service we left the Capitol and returned to the White House, where Clint and I remained throughout the evening until we were assured that Ms. Kennedy was in for the night.

Monday, November 25, was another long and emotionally draining sixteen-hour day. It was funeral day. People again lined the sidewalks along Pennsylvania Avenue that morning as we made our way to the Capitol to remove the president's body. There is a photograph of Clint and me leaving the Capitol and walking down the steps behind Mrs. Kennedy and her husband's brothers Bobby and Ted. We had another slow funeral procession past the crowd of people lining Pennsylvania Avenue back to the White House, where heads of state from around the world were waiting.

I don't know how the Secret Service was able to pull everything together and coordinate it so quickly, but they did a fantastic job. We had less than four hundred special agents located throughout the entire country. Most of them were called in to help with additional protection and security. At the same time, the Department of State handled the protection for all of the visiting dignitaries, so that involved additional State Department personnel. If that wasn't enough, all the visiting dignitaries traveled with their own protection staffs, so they had to be included too. It must have been a logistics nightmare.

To further complicate the situation, Mrs. Kennedy was making the one-and-a-quarter-mile walk, in the open, from the White House to St. Matthew's Cathedral, where a Requiem Mass was to be held. As part of Mrs. Kennedy's security detail, I walked as well. Clint and I both accompanied Mrs. Kennedy and members of the immediate family. Photographs of the day tell the story. Mrs. Kennedy walked in front with Bobby to her right and Teddy to her left. The rest of the family walked behind her. Clint was behind her on the right side. I was behind Teddy, on the left side, next to Stephen Smith. Thousands of people of all ages lined both sides of the street for the entire route.

When we arrived at St. Matthew's Cathedral, the president's casket was carried up the steps and into the church. Clint and I walked up the steps with Mrs. Kennedy as she followed behind the casket, but Clint had me stop outside the entrance while he continued inside with Mrs. Kennedy. I remained outside during the entire service.

After the Requiem Mass, I rejoined Mrs. Kennedy and the family when they exited the church. We all stood together on the steps while the president's casket was returned to the caisson. I was beside Mrs. Kennedy and John Jr., with SA Bob Foster standing directly to my left when the famous photograph of John Jr. saluting his father's casket was taken.

John F. Kennedy Jr. salutes his father's casket outside St. Matthew's Cathedral. Looking on are (left to right) Teddy, Caroline, Jackie, and Bobby Kennedy, and Special Agents Paul Landis and Bob Foster. *STRINGER / Getty Images*

When John Jr. saluted, my first thoughts were that he was shading his eyes because of the bright sun that was shining directly above us. I did not know that it was supposed to be a salute. Later I learned from SA Foster that John Jr. had become antsy during the funeral mass and that he had taken John-John into the vestibule at the rear of the cathedral to keep him occupied until the service was over. It was there that they rehearsed saluting. According to Foster, he had been teaching John Jr. how to salute ever since he and his father made a visit to Arlington National Cemetery on Veterans Day, exactly two weeks earlier.

The funeral procession from St. Matthew's Cathedral to Arlington National Cemetery is all a blur. I only remember thousands of people lining both sides of the street as we made our way toward the cemetery and across Arlington Memorial Bridge. I had to be in a car somewhere nearby, because I remember joining Clint at the cemetery and following along as President Kennedy's body was carried from the caisson up a slight incline to the grave site. I walked past the crowd of military personnel and dignitaries surrounding the grave site and took a slightly elevated position in the background. I stood by a tree and observed the service from there, but I could not hear what was being said. I was watching, trying to do my job but, in retrospect, not really there at all. What snapped me out of my malaise was the sound of approaching airplanes.

I looked to the sky and overhead, through an opening between the tree limbs, I saw dozens of air force and navy fighter jets fly by in V formations. Then I heard the more distinct sound of one particular airplane approaching. Because there was no president aboard, it did not carry the Air Force One moniker; for this flight it was just AF 26000. It was piloted by Colonel James B. Swindal, and as it passed overhead, Colonel Swindal dipped the wings of the aircraft from side to side in a final salute to our fallen president. That moment really hit me hard, and I struggled again to keep from breaking down completely. Even today I get shivers when I think about it.

The formalities continued with a twenty-one-gun salute, and I flinched at every gunshot, with visions of President Kennedy's head exploding after each one. The graveside ceremony, more than anything that had happened since the president's assassination, hit me the hardest. In retrospect that ceremony seemed to mark the beginning of the end for me as a Secret Service agent, although I did not recognize it at the time.

I have no memory of our return to the White House after the funeral services. I was wiped out both emotionally and physically. I do have a vague recollection of Clint and me returning to the grave site with Mrs. Kennedy and Bobby later that evening, but of no other activities involving Mrs. Kennedy.

When we finally finished, Clint and I walked into his office in the Map Room. All of President Kennedy's personal items that had been removed from the Oval Office earlier in the day were still there, including his famous rocking chair. We were both exhausted. Clint plopped into the chair at his desk. There was only one other place to sit. I collapsed into the former president's rocker. The last thing I remember is my two roommates, SA Dick Johnsen and SA Dave Grant, waking me during the midnight shift change and walking me to my car.

———————

A final note: AF 26000 can now be found in the National Museum of the US Air Force in Dayton, Ohio. I visited there in October 2017. Christina Douglass, the manuscript curator at the museum, gave me a personal tour of this historic plane. I was nervous and envisioned everything being the same as I remembered it from the last time that I was on board. I was surprised when I first looked where I had been sitting. The seats were gone, and in fact the entire interior of the plane had been redesigned and was completely different.

I should have known. After all, it had been nearly fifty-four years. In 1972 the plane was replaced as the regular Air Force One by another Boeing 707, but it continued to be used as a backup and had carried eight presidents in all before it was fully retired in 1998. All the seats on the side where I had been sitting had been removed and replaced with little cubicle areas, each one having a small desk and telephone. The bulkhead where I had watched Vice President Johnson take the presidential oath of office had also been relocated. Christina pointed out where the changes had been made, which helped me reconstruct what I remembered.

Christina also told me a curious story. The museum owns the logbook of all flights that Air Force One made with President Kennedy on board. On Monday November 25, 1963, as Swindal flew over the graveside, there was no president on board. No entry was made in the logbook, and there is no tangible record of that flight ever taking place.

13

ON THE MOVE, LIFE
AFTER DEATH, OR BURIED
BUT NOT FORGOTTEN

THE DAYS, NIGHTS, and weeks following President Kennedy's funeral were difficult for me. Sleepless nights were the worst. Every night when I tried to sleep, images of the assassination ran through my head. They appeared as if I was the only person in a movie theater watching everyone in Dealey Plaza, including myself, go through the same sequence of events over and over. I was there, but I wasn't there. I was completely removed. It was weird.

The events of November 22 also left me questioning my abilities as an agent as well as my self-worth, so early on I made myself a promise: if I don't feel better in six months, I'm outta here. I understood it would take a while for me to deal with what had happened. I realized that I was also exhausted, and I thought that six months would give me plenty of time to bounce back. After all, I was a special agent in the United States Secret Service. I had a reputation to uphold. I had to hang in there and "hang tough" just like the others seemed to be doing.

As close as Clint and I had become, I never told him how I felt or what was going through my mind. In fact, I don't remember either one of us ever sharing our feelings or discussing Dallas. Clint appeared to be doing fine, so I just did my best to follow his example.

Looking back, I realize that I was probably experiencing post-traumatic stress disorder (PTSD), a condition that wasn't understood at the time. As for time off, forget it. There just wasn't time for time off. We were too busy. There was too much to do, and no time for grieving. Whatever that process was about was all new to me. I just kept plugging away.

Tuesday, the day after President Kennedy's funeral, was supposed to be my day off, but I had to work. At least I got to sleep in and didn't report to the White House until 1:00 PM. At some point during the afternoon, Mrs. Kennedy, Bobby Kennedy, and Clint took a White House limo to Arlington National Cemetery, while I followed in a separate car. I remember making another visit to Arlington with Mrs. Kennedy, Caroline, John Jr., and the two dogs, Charlie and Clipper. I have no entry in my memo book as to when this visit occurred, but I do remember watching all of them pile into a station wagon at the White House, following them to Arlington, and parking behind them at the cemetery. I'm thinking Bobby was also along too, but I can't verify that. I don't remember who drove their wagon or who was in the follow-up car with me. I do remember it was dark and we parked behind them. The headlights from our car lit up the inside of the wagon, and I could see Caroline through the rear window and the two dogs jumping around in the back. The doors opened, and the dogs were off and running. I remember thinking how disrespectful I thought it was to allow the dogs to run loose in the cemetery while everyone visited the president's grave site.

After a short visit, everyone, including the dogs, piled back into the wagon, and we returned to the White House. That's all I remember about that visit, and I'm not even sure if it occurred that evening. All I have listed in my memo book for that Tuesday is "On duty at White House and Arlington Cemetery." That was the only activity of the day for me.

I spent Wednesday at the White House, and on Thursday, Thanksgiving morning, I was on an 8:30 AM flight to Hyannis Port, Massachusetts, where I spent a long, dreary weekend at the Kennedy Compound.

After we returned to Washington on Sunday, December 1, Mrs. Kennedy started to get serious about moving. President Johnson had given her until the end of the week to organize her affairs and move out of the White House. It hadn't occurred to me that the next few days would also be my last days on the White House Detail. Clint was the one who brought that to my attention.

At first, I didn't understand what he was telling me. We were still assigned to Mrs. Kennedy—or were we? In my mind, Mrs. Kennedy would always be the First Lady, but we were no longer going to be in the White House, and there was no law that required former First Ladies to receive Secret Service protection. What was going to happen to us after Mrs. Kennedy left the White House? What was going to happen to me? These were the questions on my mind during the next few days. There was no guarantee what my next assignment would even be.

President Johnson helped resolve those issues. At his request, Congress passed new legislation allowing the protection of Mrs. Kennedy, Caroline, and John Jr. to continue for the next two years (Public Law 83-195). Clint and I would remain with Mrs. Kennedy but on a separate detail, no longer a part of the White House Detail. However, we would still have use of the security office located off the West Wing to type our daily reports, etc.

On Friday, December 6, Mrs. Kennedy and the children finally moved out of the White House and took up temporary residence at the home of Averell and Marie Harriman at 3038 N Street NW in Georgetown. The Harrimans were friends of the Kennedys, and Averell Harriman had served as ambassador-at-large in the Kennedy administration.

In mid-December, Mrs. Kennedy took the children to Palm Beach for a three-week visit with their grandfather, Joe Kennedy, over the Christmas and New Year holidays. The weather was nice, but the mood was gloomy. I could not get the assassination out of my mind, and Clint and I didn't talk about it. After returning to Georgetown, Mrs. Kennedy took possession of her own new home at 3017 N Street NW, only a few houses down and across the street from the Harriman residence.

Moving day for Mrs. Kennedy was not quite what I expected. Clint and I spent all day Thursday, January 16, driving between the Harriman home, the White House storage facility, and her new home in Georgetown. That evening she did not settle in like I thought she would either. The three of us, Mrs. Kennedy, Clint, and I, caught a Northeast Airlines flight to Boston, where Clint and I spent the next three days escorting Mrs. Kennedy around the Boston area and Senator Ted Kennedy's residence.

When we returned to Georgetown, Mrs. Kennedy and the children were still living out of the Harriman residence. They did not move into her new home until February 1, 1964. Clint and I set up shop in our cars parked on the street in front of the house. For me, it felt like guarding the Eisenhower grandchildren in Gettysburg all over again, working out of a car.

One week after Mrs. Kennedy moved into her new home, we were off again. She certainly wasn't letting any grass grow under her feet. We went to Palm Beach for three days, returned to DC for two days, then off to New York City and the Carlyle Hotel for two more days, back to DC for a half day, and then on to her new house in Atoka, Virginia, which Mrs. Kennedy now referred to as Wexford, named for the Irish birthplace of the Kennedy ancestors.

When we first moved out of the White House, and when I had the occasion to drive Mrs. Kennedy, either alone or with the children, it was especially tough. Driving the car, the soft sobs coming from the backseat or the unanswerable questions from the children were hard to ignore. There was nothing I could say or do, and it wasn't my place to do anything. It broke my heart, and I had a hard time holding back tears myself.

Today, people talk about grieving and counseling. In 1964, not only was I unaware of what grieving was all about, but professional counseling wasn't even a possibility. Men didn't do that. That's the way it was, and that's the way I felt. There was no way that I was going to talk to someone else about my feelings or disclose any weaknesses.

The gawkers didn't help. Everywhere we went, they were there. *Why don't you just leave her alone?* I wanted to scream. Meanwhile, the politicians, the general public, and everyone else you could imagine were demanding answers. All sorts of rumors and conspiracy theories began to emerge and were constantly being reported in the newspapers, on the radio, or on television. It was impossible not to think about the assassination. We just kept busy and on the move.

Mrs. Kennedy set the pattern for our days early on. When she went into mourning, she didn't just sit around. She kept busy and on the move. There were things to do, places to go, and people to see. This fit her style and was nothing new, but it also meant that there was no break or rest period for us. *The busier the better* seemed to work for me at the time. It helped keep my mind off Texas.

After reviewing the memorandum books, which I still have stored in a safe deposit box, I found only one period when Mrs. Kennedy spent ten straight days at her new home in Georgetown, a home that had acquired the name Camelot. (At one point

there is a shift in how I describe my location in my daily nota-
tions from "on duty Kennedy residence" to "on duty Camelot.")
The rest of the time we were on the move, traveling from place
to place.

The following five months were a blur of places and events.
We made trips to New York City and stayed at the Carlyle. We
went to Boston and stayed at the Ritz. Plus, there were trips to
Palm Beach and to Wexford in Virginia. Throughout this time,
my scheduled days off were Fridays and Saturdays. But we were
on the move so much that getting my regular days off was the
exception rather than the rule.

On Wednesday, February 19, we traveled from Washington to
Atlanta, where we picked up an official car to take us to Thomasville, Georgia, for a stay at Greenwood Plantation, one of the
homes of John H. "Jock" Whitney, the former ambassador to
Britain and owner of the *New York Herald Tribune*. According to
my notebook, we arrived at the plantation early in the morning
of February 20. I stopped work at 2:00 AM but was back at work
at 8:00 AM. I don't remember what we did, and I don't remember where Clint and I stayed, but we were there for a long, five-
day weekend. For the return flight to DC we flew nonstop from
Thomasville in Whitney's private aircraft.

On March 26, 1964, Mrs. Kennedy and the children went skiing in Stowe, Vermont. None of the agents assigned to Mrs. Kennedy and the children knew how to ski. There was, however,
one agent on the White House Detail who knew how to ski: SA
Dick Johnsen, my roommate. We recruited him to come along
to assist with protection. We all flew to Burlington, Vermont,
on the *Caroline* and drove from there to Stowe. All of us who
couldn't ski took lessons, and we spent three days practicing our
newly learned skills on Mount Mansfield while keeping an eye
on Mrs. Kennedy and the children.

After departing Vermont, the *Caroline* headed to New York City—not DC, which I thought was the original plan. Mrs. Kennedy was going to spend the night at the Carlyle Hotel, and Caroline and John Jr. were continuing on to Georgetown without her. This was all news to me. *Plus*, I learned that the following morning Mrs. Kennedy was going to leave for Antigua in the British West Indies.

My first thought was *Wow, how neat*; however, I soon realized that I had a problem. When I packed for Vermont and skiing, I had only packed winter clothes. I had no warm-weather clothing with me. This was definitely an issue. I would not only be uncomfortable but also look pretty silly walking around the tropics in winter clothes and snow boots. Luckily my roommate Dick was still with us. He was returning to Washington with Caroline, John Jr., and the Kiddie Detail. I asked him to throw some of my clean underwear, fresh socks, polo shirts, a blazer, and anything else he could think of into a suitcase and have it sent to wherever I ended up.

"Wherever" turned out to be Half Moon Bay, Antigua, where Clint and I checked into the Half Moon Bay Hotel, another famous location where we stayed for five dollars a night. (Author's note: The original Half Moon Bay Hotel where Clint and I stayed was a favorite landing spot for Audrey Hepburn and Elton John. It was destroyed by Hurricane Luis in 1995.) Mrs. Kennedy stayed with her friend Mrs. "Bunny" Mellon at her nearby Mill Reef Club estate. I felt pretty self-conscious that first day in Antigua hanging around the hotel and the Mill Reef Club in winter clothes, but my roommate came through, and by that evening after work, a suitcase full of warm-weather clothing was waiting for me at the hotel.

Wherever Clint and I went, we always made friends with the staff. They helped keep us informed of any surprise activities that were in the early planning stages. They didn't know it, but they were our undercover agents. Also, we seldom went hungry. One of the young housekeepers who worked for Mrs. Mellon happened to be getting married while we were in Antigua. On the day before her wedding, she was excitedly telling us about a party she was having that night at her home. She said that the two of us were welcome to stop by, and she gave Clint the directions. We knew that if we went, we would be late because of our workday, in addition to the time it would take to clean up and change clothes afterward. But when we did finish, I said to Clint, "Let's do it. I think she'll be surprised to see us."

Clint had the directions and was driving. The road we were on was either dirt or gravel, I don't remember which, but I do remember it was dark and the road was barely wide enough for one car. The only light came from our headlights boring through the darkness, and the only things visible were the road and sugar cane, and lots of it. Ten-to-twelve-foot-high stalks of sugar cane that grew right up to the edges of and along both sides of the road. It was so dark, it almost felt like we were driving through a tunnel. There were no road signs for directions or any other sign of life.

We were in the middle of nowhere, and after a few miles, I was beginning to wonder if Clint had missed a turn somewhere along the way and if we were lost. I was riding in the front passenger seat, and I turned to him and said, "You know, Clint, if something happened to us out here, it would probably be a month before anyone ever found us. Even if they ever did find us, I doubt if they would ever learn what happened to us." Clint agreed, and assured me we weren't lost and continued driving, but it was really spooky.

We finally reached a landmark that Clint recognized from the directions, and he turned down a narrow dirt driveway. The house at the end of the driveway wasn't much to look at, more like a shotgun shack, not quite what Clint and I had become accustomed to in our travels. The only other people there were family, and Clint and I were the only two White people. I think our lady friend was surprised that we actually showed up. She just bubbled over with excitement, and our warm reception by everyone there overshadowed anything else. I don't think many other people would have gone out of their way to do what Clint and I did that night, and I'm glad we did it.

On our way back to Half Moon Bay Hotel, I wondered what kind of a life the newlyweds would have together. I was feeling good about our adventure through the sugar cane, but I was also feeling melancholy at the same time. I don't know how to explain it. When I went to bed that night, the thoughts of the evening dissipated, and when I closed my eyes . . . I was back in Dealey Plaza.

After returning to Georgetown from Antigua, I finally had a day off, but that was hardly time enough to catch my breath. Three days later the beat continued. Mrs. Kennedy, Clint, and I were off again, this time to Boston. We stayed at the Ritz and spent four days traveling between the hotel, Ted Kennedy's residence, and Harvard University. From Boston we went directly to New York City for an additional three days of shopping before returning home to Georgetown.

Toward the end of April 1964, Mrs. Kennedy took Caroline and John Jr. to New York City. She stayed at the Carlyle, and the children stayed with their cousins Stephen and William Smith, who lived a couple of blocks away on Fifth Avenue. We all went to the World's Fair.

After leaving New York City, we returned to Camelot in Georgetown for a whole three hours before leaving again for Wexford in Atoka. Two days later we returned to Camelot. We spent the following ten days in Georgetown. This was the longest stretch of time that I'd spent at one location since President Kennedy's assassination in November 1963.

It was now early May 1964, and my self-imposed six-month decision whether or not to leave the Secret Service was at hand. Until then I hadn't had time to think about leaving. Now I had the time to think. My nights were still haunted by the events of the assassination. I decided that maybe if I left the Secret Service and the constant reminders of Dallas, the bad dreams would stop. I didn't tell Clint what I was planning. I didn't confer with anyone.

On Wednesday May 6, I had a day off, but I drove into the White House, went into the Secret Service office off the West Wing, sat down at the desk designated for our use, and typed my thirty-day resignation notice. Agents wandered in and out of the office while I was there, but no one paid any attention to what I was doing. I finished my letter, signed it, and dropped it in the outbox and left.

In the following two weeks, Mrs. Kennedy made trips to Bedford Village, New York; New York City; and Boston (two trips); and a side trip to Hyannis Port. I began to wonder if I had made the right decision. I loved the travel—I loved being on the move. I loved the excitement and the adrenaline rushes. I loved my job. The Secret Service was giving me the opportunity to do what I wanted to do, and to be where I wanted to be. I didn't want to be assigned outside of Washington. I knew that I could eventually return to the White House Detail after Mrs. Kennedy's detail, if that's what I wanted, but that wasn't my issue.

My issue was that I had begun to question my abilities as a Secret Service agent. I felt I was not up to the task. I compared myself to other agents and felt insecure. I focused on the negatives of my job and not the positives. Added to this were the constant reminders of Dallas and the ever-present nightmares. I still couldn't or wouldn't talk to Clint about my situation, even though I considered him my best friend. Clint appeared to be doing just fine, trucking along like nothing ever bothered him, doing his job as usual, always the professional. At the time I had no way of knowing that he was suffering too. We probably would have ended up bawling our eyes out together if either of us had had the courage to open up.

I'd made my decision, and I was stubborn. I wasn't about to back down or go back on my word. My father had always stressed the importance of commitment. Commitment to me meant being on time for a date or meeting a deadline. It also meant keeping my word and following through once I'd made a decision. I had made a commitment to leave the Secret Service, and I wasn't about to back down.

I'd been in the service for nearly five years. In June I accompanied Clint and Mrs. Kennedy to New York City on one last trip. On Friday, June 12, 1964, we returned to Georgetown, and I made my last entry into my last memorandum book: "6 PM discontinued." These were the words I wrote whenever I finished a day's work, but now those words had more meaning. I was done—but not quite done. I had almost a month of unused annual leave.

I don't remember much about that last month. I was on paid vacation, so I took advantage of whatever I could before my time was up. President Johnson made a trip to New York City, and I hopped on the round-trip flight with the agents who made the trip. I got strange looks, but no one ever questioned why I was there. I drove to Cape Cod and stayed in a rented cottage with the agents on the Caroline and John Jr. Kiddie Detail who were there for the summer.

Three days after my twenty-ninth birthday, on August 15, 1964, I officially left the Secret Service.

For Paul Landis —
with deep appreciation for all your help
to us for three years
Jacqueline Kennedy

Autographed photo of Mrs. Kennedy that Paul Landis received on his last day of work, Friday, June 12, 1964. *Author's collection*

EPILOGUE

I DIDN'T READ THE WARREN COMMISSION REPORT until 2018, almost fifty-four years after it was first published. I never felt like I needed to read anything about that day. I was in Dallas in November 1963. I witnessed President Kennedy's assassination in person. I was at Parkland Memorial Hospital. I was in Trauma Room #1. I didn't need to read about the gruesome details or conspiracy theories. I was there.

I was also stubborn and in denial. I didn't want to stir up the vivid memories that I had finally suppressed for so many years. The Warren Commission had long ago concluded their investigation into President Kennedy's assassination. I considered that their report had to be accurate and credible, even though I had never read it. The fact that I was never called to testify before the Warren Commission didn't bother me. At the time, I was thankful. I dreaded the thought of having to testify, knowing that I would have broken down and cried. Not a pretty sight for a special agent in the United States Secret Service.

Why was I never called to testify? That question had always lingered in the back of my mind until I learned, years later, that Clint Hill was the only one of the eight agents in the follow-up car who was called, likely because he was the only agent to make it to the president's limo.

After leaving the Secret Service, I moved to Cape Cod, Massachusetts, in late summer 1964. I intended to make my fortune in real estate. My timing wasn't the best, and I soon learned that waterfront property was not a top priority in the middle of a Cape Cod winter.

I moved to New York City and did some modeling and worked in film production, eventually forming my own company, Landis/Wolf Inc. We produced television commercials, and our first commercial won a Clio in the American TV Commercials Festival in 1967. We also produced the first Trac II commercial for Gillette's test market and the first Subaru commercials introducing front-wheel-drive automobiles to the American public.

I was married and starting to raise a family when my wife, Carolyn, and I decided Ohio was a better place to raise children than Millwood, New York. Another impetus for the move was the morning I saw a commuter drop dead of a heart attack while running to catch a train during the early morning rush. In 1975, my wife, daughter Jennifer, and I moved to Chesterland, Ohio, near Cleveland. I went to work for Knutsen Machine Products Inc., the business of Carolyn's uncle and father. Our son, Tom, was born three years later.

In 1979 I received a telephone call from someone representing the House Select Committee on Assassinations, led by Congressman Louis Stokes to reinvestigate the findings in the Warren Commission report. During the entire fifteen years prior to that call, I hadn't looked at my written report. Though I was never formally called to testify, my written report still exists. I dug my copy out of a storage box and reviewed it. I found some errors in my wording, but nothing to change my recollection that I had heard three shots and that they all had come from behind me, probably from the Texas School Book Depository. One shooter, three shots, period. The report was factual but not overly descriptive.

Though my written report discussed the shooting, I never mentioned the bullet I had found on the seat of the presidential limo. It didn't seem an important detail to mention at the time. I had no way of knowing that Exhibit 399, also referred to as the "third bullet," would become a source of controversy. Once I'd left the bullet on the president's gurney, I forgot about it. I'd done my job. I had saved and prevented an important piece of evidence from becoming lost, and I assumed at the time it would be found where I placed it. I never thought about that bullet again until the evening of March 14, 2014, when I picked up *Six Seconds in Dallas*.

Throughout my life, not only did I resist thinking about the assassination, but I also told myself that I would never go back to Dallas. In 1983 I changed my mind and returned for the annual convention of the Association of Former Agents of the US Secret Service (AFAUSSS). Despite my anxieties, I decided the convention was a good excuse to return and walk around Dealey Plaza and the School Book Depository. I hoped the visit would put my mind at ease. It didn't, although if people asked, I would assure them that it had helped. It was just easier to tell them what they wanted to hear.

At the time, I was also going through a protracted divorce. After the divorce became final in 1984, I remained with Knutsen Machine Products for eight more years. Then I left the company and ran my own successful house-painting business and never really thought much about my time in the Secret Service. People who knew about my past would sometimes ask about the Kennedys, but I never talked about the assassination. The only real connection with my past life was an occasional Christmas card from Barbara Anne Eisenhower Flöttl.

I have lived most of my life with a tunnel-vision view of the events of November 22, 1963. We, the agents who were there, wrote reports, but we did not talk about our experiences with one another. Only in recent years did I learn that my roommate Special Agent Dick Johnsen had been given the recovered bullet I found by the director of security for Parkland Hospital. In the aftermath of events, one gurney (presumed to be Connally's) was taken from an elevator and another was already in the elevator lobby when the bullet was discovered by a hospital employee, Darrell Tomlinson. When Tomlinson moved the gurney already in the lobby against the wall, the bullet emerged from under the mat. Tomlinson gave the bullet to the security director, who gave it to Dick. Dick mentions this in his report to the Warren Commission, but at the time we never spoke about the events of November 22, and I didn't read his report until I began writing this book.

Over the past twenty years, I have been contacted on more than one occasion as anniversaries of the assassination approached, or about the Warren Commission's work, but I had little interest in talking about the events of November 22 from my own perspective.

In 2007 Jerry Blaine contacted me regarding a book he intended to write called *The Kennedy Detail*. I had no interest in participating and forgot about it. A couple of years later Jerry contacted me again. He brought me up to date and told me that Clint Hill was editing his book for accuracy. Last chance. I trusted Clint, and I agreed to participate. Jerry's coauthor, Lisa McCubbin, contacted me, and we did telephone interviews.

After the publication of Jerry and Lisa's book in 2010, the Discovery Channel produced a documentary about *The Kennedy Detail*. I participated and openly shared my painful inner feelings. That's when I discovered, for the first time, that I was not alone.

Clint then collaborated with Lisa McCubbin himself on two books, *Mrs. Kennedy and Me* (2012) and *Five Days in November* (2013). I attended presentations for both that they made at the Henry Ford Museum in Dearborn, Michigan. (The museum houses the Kennedy limo and the follow-up car in its collection.) During Clint's presentation for *Five Days*, he mentioned something about a "missing bullet." My ears perked up, but I didn't say anything. I knew nothing about a missing bullet.

By 2013, I was beginning to speak more openly about my Secret Service career, and about President Kennedy's assassination. Little circumstantial things were happening. It's as if there was gold dust in the air, and sudden opportunities began to present themselves—opportunities that might have seemed coincidental if it weren't for the fact that the whole world had opened up. More information was coming out, and more people were interested in revisiting the events of November 22, 1963.

Art Greenberg, a friend from Bally's gym, worked for WAKR, one of the talk radio stations near my home in northeast Ohio. He asked me if I would do a radio interview as the fiftieth anniversary of JFK's assassination approached. I agreed.

On November 22, 2013, I did an unrehearsed phone interview on WKAR. It was with someone I didn't know and couldn't see, and I felt uncomfortable while doing it. One of the people who heard the interview was Lew Merletti.

During the presidency of Bill Clinton, Merletti was the nineteenth director of the United States Secret Service. After retiring from the service in 1999, Merletti accepted a position as senior vice president with the Cleveland Browns—in charge of security, naturally. At the time of my radio interview, Merletti lived in Beachwood, Ohio, just a few miles from my house. He and an attorney friend, Jim Kersey, were having lunch together that day, and Lew was telling Jim about my interview, which he'd heard while driving to work that morning. Lew told me later that he turned to Jim and said, "I've been in Cleveland all these years and here's this guy who lives here, too, and we've never met. I've got to talk to him." A moment later the world proved even smaller when Kersey replied, "I know him—he bought a house in Chesterland, Ohio, from my sister. I'll see if I can get his number."

Merletti called me and we got together. We exchanged war stories and became friends.

It was later, in March 2014, when I started to read the book Chief Lee from the Shaker Heights Police Department had given me, *Six Seconds in Dallas*. As events recounted in the introduction to this book illustrate, I had not realized until that moment, reading that book, that there was an error in the Warren Commission report.

Though I had not read the Warren Commission report, I knew that there had been a lot of criticisms, and *Six Seconds in Dallas* author Josiah Thompson was doing his own "micro-study" of the evidence. I was reading along, thinking that his account was fairly accurate to what I saw and remembered, when I came to page 146. Thompson was describing a "Super Bullet" that, according to the commission, was found on Governor Connally's stretcher and had caused his wounds. This is where my heart skipped a beat, and I first realized that the Warren Commission's report was wrong: The "Super Bullet" hadn't been on Governor Connally's stretcher in Trauma Room #2. I recognized it as the bullet I had found in the limo and placed next to President Kennedy's feet in Trauma Room #1.

The day after I started reading *Six Seconds in Dallas*, I began to make notes. Because the information was sensitive to me and because I wasn't ready to share it yet, I opened a safe deposit box at a local bank and placed my notes and records inside.

When I finally decided to share my information with Lew Merletti, I knew everything I said would be held in confidence. Merletti's response to my revelation was immediate, and he encouraged me to tell my story to Ken Gormley, dean of the School of Law at Duquesne University (now the thirteenth president of the university) and the author of *The Death of American Virtue: Clinton vs. Starr*. Gormley had interviewed Merletti during the Monica Lewinsky scandal that led to President Clinton's impeachment. Merletti trusted Gormley. I repeated my story to Gormley, and he agreed with Merletti: "You have a story here that needs to be told."

This is the story I kept buried—even from myself—for more than fifty years. For five decades I couldn't bring myself to review the events of November 22, 1963, in detail. Everyone but me seemed to have read the Warren Commission report. I just accepted that whatever conclusions the commission had drawn had to be accurate and true.

In this book I have shared what I saw, what I did, and only what I know to be factual about that fateful November weekend. As soon as I completed writing my story and typed "The End," tears started rolling down my cheeks for no apparent reason. I just sat staring at my computer as the tears flowed uncontrollably, dripping off of my chin for the next ten minutes. I just couldn't stop crying. It was as if the safety valve on a pressure cooker had finally burst open, releasing all the suppressed feelings and emotions that I had kept buried for so long.

This is my story.

INDEX